Test Drive Blender

A Starter Manual for New Users

Test Drive Blender

A Starter Manual for New Users

John M. Blain

CRC Press
Taylor & Francis Group
Boca Raton   London   New York

CRC Press is an imprint of the
Taylor & Francis Group, an **informa** business

CRC Press
Taylor & Francis Group
6000 Broken Sound Parkway NW, Suite 300
Boca Raton, FL 33487-2742

© 2017 by Taylor & Francis Group, LLC
CRC Press is an imprint of Taylor & Francis Group, an Informa business

No claim to original U.S. Government works

Printed in Canada on acid-free paper
Version Date: 20161011

International Standard Book Number-13: 978-1-4987-9914-0 (Paperback)
International Standard Book Number-13: 978-1-1386-2879-3 (Hardback)

Visit the Taylor & Francis Web site at
http://www.taylorandfrancis.com

and the CRC Press Web site at
http://www.crcpress.com

Computer Requirements
for
BLENDER

To run Blender, your computer must meet a minimum specification.

Hang on! Don't close the book. Read on.

The minimum (basic usage) requirement is:

32-bit dual core 2 GHz CPU with SSE2 support

2 GB RAM

24 bits 1280 × 768 display

Mouse or trackpad

OpenGL 2.1 compatible graphics with 512 MB RAM.

This specification pretty much applies to most off the shelf laptop computers which retail in the lower price range. You should therefore be good to go with most personal computers (PCs). Of course, the bigger the better and that certainly applies to the monitor display. There is a lot of info on the Blender interface so the bigger the screen the better. If you have a small laptop, hook it up to a reasonably sized monitor and I would recommend plugging in a USB wheel mouse. This gives a more enjoyable experience.

Test Drive
BLENDER

Discover Computer Graphics

Take a test drive in **Blender** and discover what's under the hood. The power is fantastic, the controls will take you to places you never dreamed of, and what you can create is limited only by your imagination.

Go! Take a test drive and get hooked on **Blender**. Become a Blenderhead and create fantastic **Computer Graphics**.

This book will introduce you to the controls and steer you toward understanding what **Blender** can do. The program is a fantastic application with which you can create 3D (three-dimensional) models of objects and characters. The objects and characters can be placed in scenes. The scenes are captured by camera and rendered into digital images. The objects and characters can be animated and then, again, captured by camera and rendered to video files. Video files are then compiled into movies.

This book will show you how to make the **Blender** program go through some of its paces and give you an insight into this fantastic world. You will be shown the controls and given operation instructions allowing you to activate a variety of Blender's features.

Blender is crammed full of features and the trick is to be aware of them and learn how to combine the features to do what you want.

The book does not attempt to show you everything. It cannot. There is far far too much. The book contains merely a sample of what the program can do. It's like opening the corner of a box of chocolates and selecting a few yummy pieces to taste. You can get hooked on chocolate. You can get hooked on **Blender**. After trying a sample, I'm sure you will want to continue munching and discover everything there is. Like chocolate, you can never have enough.

It is hoped that you will become interested and encouraged to pursue the world of computer modeling and animation using **Blender**.

Blender Splash Screens

At each new release, Blender displays a new Splash Screen.

Contents

Try out an animation project combining several Blender features to make something fly, blow up, and catch on fire.

If you didn't know how, this is where you find out how to download and install Blender on your Windows Computer.

Look under the hood and discover more about Blender.

See a summary of the Blender windows, which gives you an insight into what you can do with the program.

When you get stuck into Blender and begin to tinker inside you will need a manual to help you, and tutorials to guide you.

Acknowledgments

In compiling this book I have used Blender files and artworks sourced on the Internet. These resources serve to demonstrate the wonderful array of computer graphics materials that are available.

For the book cover: The front cover of the book is compiled using a screen capture from the Blender website of Yo Frankie! and an image titled Violet created by Lucas Falcao.

In the Introduction: A screen capture from Yo Frankie! has been used again.

Image obtained from the Blender website: www.blender.org

Also in the Introduction: To demonstrate artwork;

Red Car image created by: Linolafett

Young Lady image created by: Lucas Falcao

Young Man Levi created by: Yusuf Umar

In describing how to view Blender, Features and Demo Reels screen captures from the Blender website have been used.

Throughout the book I have used clip art sourced from various websites offering Open Source images free for use for any purpose including commercial applications.

Author

Hi! My name is John.

I was born in England, in the county of Wiltshire, in the town of Swindon in 1942. I have written this book in 2016, so you can do the math and figure out my age.

You may well ask, what's an old dude doing writing a book on how to run a computer graphics program?

PCs certainly weren't around when I was a kid. Neither were televisions nor mobile phones. Most people didn't have a telephone in their home and most people didn't have a car. When I was born the bombs were still dropping during the World War II and they didn't stop until a couple of years later.

I had a poorly start, as a kid, got sick and spent a lot of time in hospital. When I went to school I discovered I couldn't spell but I could draw pictures and I could make things. At 10-years old I emigrated to Canada with my family and went through school in British Columbia. I continued to draw and tried my hand at wood carving. There's a lot of wood in British Columbia. Following school I returned to England by myself and became an apprentice to an engineering company. Being an apprentice meant you signed a contract for 5 years and worked and studied to become something useful in life. Boy, you sure worked and I learned to do what I was told. I'm not too sure if I ever became useful but I became a draughtsman and spent my life drawing and making things.

When I finished my apprenticeship I returned to Canada and worked in Vancouver for several months. This proved to be a mere stepping stone in life's journey since I made the big jump to a life down under in Australia. I continued drafting, did further studies, and graduated to designing. I couldn't escape from wood. I eventually became a sales engineer in sawmill machinery manufacturing.

In all of my working life there were no computers. Engineering calculations were assisted by using a slide rule and trigonometric tables. You can Google those to find out what they are. My only computer at work was a scientific calculator.

When retired I had to find something to do. I tried woodcarving for a while. Won a few prizes, didn't make any money but had fun.

Then I discovered the computer and Blender with all its buttons and panels and sliders and windows, which were a mystery. Engineering is about solving mysteries so I began solving the mysteries of Blender and thought I would save you some time by passing on what I have discovered.

I think Blender is a fantastic program that allows you to be creative in the modern world. Have a go.

Happy Blending.

What Is Blender?

Blender is a computer graphics program for making three-dimensional (3D) models of characters and objects. The characters and objects are placed in scenes like the one shown in the picture above. Parts of the scene are captured as digital images or a series of images then rendered into image files or video. The scene in the picture is from a Blender game called Yo Frankie!

You can make computer games with Blender.

What Is Computer Graphics?

Computer graphics is the process of using a computer to make still pictures and moving pictures just like all the ads and cartoons you see on TV. You also use computer graphics to make games like the ones on your i-pad or i-phone.

Yes! You can make your own games.

How Much Does Blender Cost?

Blender is absolutely **FREE!** It doesn't cost anything. You can download the program and use it for anything you wish.

Amazing Images Made with Blender

Image created by: Linolafett

Image created by: Yusuf Umar

Image created by: Lucas Falcao

It's easy to show you pictures in a book but not so easy to show you examples of video.

Grab your computer and head over to the **Blender** website to see some fantastic demo reels.

www.blender.org

This is the website where you get the program. When you are on the Blender page, click on **Features** in the border at the top. It's not surprising that some of Blender's fantastic features are shown on the next page that opens. To see the video demonstrations click on **Demo Reels** in the header just below the big colored window at the top of the page. Click on the little white triangle in any of the windows and see some amazing stuff.

Cycles Render Engine Reel 2015

Cycles Render Engine Reel 2014

How Do I Get Blender?

You can download the Blender program from the same website where you found the Demo Reel.

If you know how to download and install programs, you won't want to read through a whole bunch of instructions so I have put these at the back of the book. If you need some help with downloading, read through the instruction page and if you need to, ask for help.

Hi! My name is Shannon. I will be giving you tips here and there.

Why Shannon?

Shannon is an old Irish name for Wise Owl.

When you have the program installed, you are ready to find out how to drive Blender. It's like learning to drive a car. You have to know which buttons and pedals to push to make it do what you want and Blender has a lot of pedals.

Learning to drive will get you used to reading and following the instructions. This is very important since I write in a peculiar way. You have to be peculiar to write this stuff.

Before I start the driving lesson on how to drive the program, I have to assume that you know how to drive the computer. The computer can be a PC or a laptop but it is preferable that you have a **keyboard**—and a **mouse**.

Like! As if we don't know what a keyboard and mouse look like.

Blender is designed to be operated using a keyboard and a three-button mouse. The mouse can be a wheel mouse. That's the one with a scroll wheel in the middle which acts as a middle mouse button (MMB). You can use the laptop touch pad but you will have to learn special keystrokes to do this. I recommend you connect a mouse to your laptop.

Start Your Engine

OK! You have Blender installed. Place your mouse cursor on the desktop icon and give it a double click with the left mouse button (LMB).

The Mouse Cursor

Desktop Icon

This Is What You See

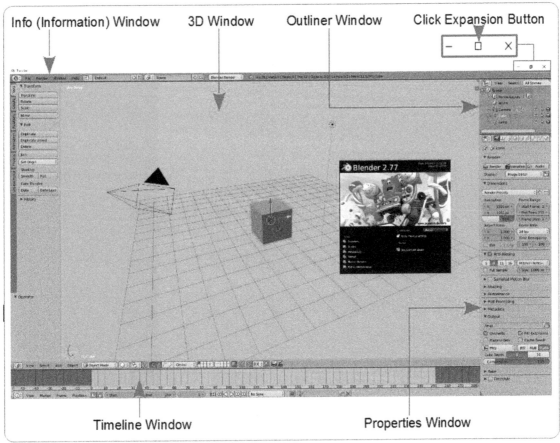

Blender Windows—The Graphical User Interface (GUI)

If Blender doesn't open full size on your screen, click the Expansion button.

I told you Blender has a lot of buttons and pedals. We call the pedals things like Windows, Panels, Headers, Buttons, Sliders, Selection Drop Down Menus, etc. There is a lot of "et cetera." **Don't Freak Out!** You will soon get the hang of it.

The Blender Screen Arrangement

The **Start Screen** shows five different **Windows** with a **Splash Screen** in the middle. The splash screen shows you what version of BLENDER you have and gives you some links to websites.

When you click with your mouse cursor in the **3D Window,** the Splash Screen disappears.

Blender is updated regularly as the developers tweak and improve things and add more fantastic features. Each time the program is updated, the Splash Screen is changed so you know what version you have. The program doesn't update automatically. You have to visit the Blender website and download and install the new version.

What Are Windows?

Windows are the different panels into which the screen is divided. They have nothing to do with the "Windows Operating System" which allows you to run the Blender program. You may be running a different operating system. The different Windows are:

The 3D Window—This is the main workspace which is a view of a 3D World.

The Info (Information) Window—Gives you access to controls.

The Outliner Window—Shows you a list of everything in the 3D Window.

The Timeline Window—Is where you set up and operate animations.

The Properties Window—Contains information about things in the 3D Window.

Don't be concerned about the detail of what all the Windows with all the buttons do at this point. Everyone finds the arrangement confusing when they first see it. Blender can do lots and lots of things so you would expect lots and lots of buttons. As you can see there are lots and lots. As you work through the book, the windows and buttons will be explained as you need to know them.

When you start something new, you always have heaps of questions. Don't feel confused. Think about all the fun things you are going to learn. Keep following along and we will sort things out.

Take a Look at the 3D Window

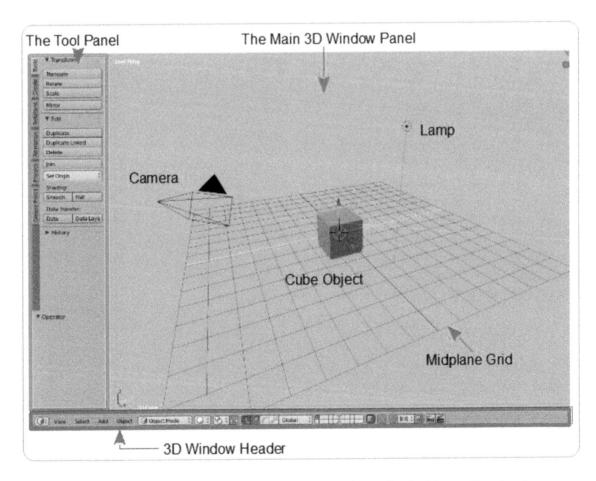

Now that doesn't look so bad when you take a closer look. It's pretty simple.

The **3D Window** is divided into three panels. The main **3D Windo**w where you do the work. The **Tool Panel** and the **Header** contain buttons and subpanels where you click your mouse to access settings for things in the 3D Window.

In the 3D Window Main Panel you see that there is a **Cube Object,** a **Lamp,** and a **Camera**. There is also a **Midplane Grid**.

The Camera will take a picture of whatever it is pointed at in the 3D Space. The 3D Space is very dark without some lighting so a Lamp is provided for illumination. The Midplane Grid gives you a reference for placing things in the 3D Space. Imagine being in real space far away from the nearest planet or star. It would be nice to have a grid to know which way is up and how far away from something you were.

If you look closely at the grid, you will see there is a green line at the center running from left to right and a red line running from the back to the front. These are the X and Y axes. There is another axis which is the Z axis (not shown) which runs up and down in space. You see all three axes in the lower left-hand corner of the main window panel.

Let's Do Something!

I know you are just raring to go and push some buttons and make something happen so let's do something just to give you a feel. This is going to change your 3D Window view so we will show you how to get back to square one when you mess up. This is a good thing to know.

The Cube Object in your 3D Window will look like this. The orange outline shows that the Cube is selected. It has red, green, and blue arrows pointing away from its center. This arrow arrangement is the **Manipulation Widget.**

What's a **Widget**? I saw that one coming.

The Oxford Dictionary says a widget is any small device that you do not know the name of. Not very helpful is it? I guess it must be the same as a thingamyjig or a whatsit.

The Widget in our case lets you move something about in 3D Space, keeping in a straight line. Try it out. Place your mouse cursor on any of the arrows, click LMB, hold and drag the mouse in the direction of the arrow. Release the mouse button to set the cube in its new position. Click and drag in the opposite direction.

Look at the 3D Window Header. The Widget has different modes. Try them out.

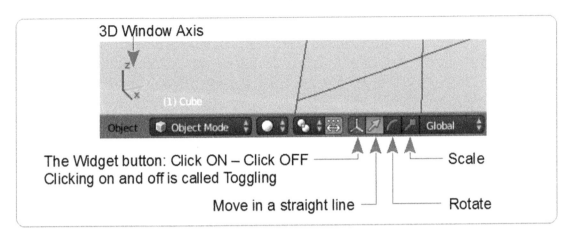

3D Window Axis

(1) Cube

The Widget button: Click ON – Click OFF
Clicking on and off is called Toggling

Move in a straight line

Scale

Rotate

You can also move the **Cube Object** freely by pressing the **G Key** on the keyboard, dragging the mouse then clicking LMB to release. **G** stands for Grab.

One thing to note here is the **Cube Object** has an orange outline (we call this the Default Cube since it appears by default when you start a new BLENDER Scene). The outline indicates that this Object is selected. When you have more than one Object in a scene, you have to select the one you want to work on. You select an Object by clicking with the right mouse button (RMB). The orange outline appears. To deselect an Object, press the A key on the keyboard.

Note: If you press the A Key to deselect an Object, then press the A Key a second time, you will select all the Objects in the Scene. Press A to deselect.

More Moving About

Let's really get the scene scrambled. Look at the **Num Pad** (Number Pad) on the keyboard. The Num Pad can be used to rotate the 3D Window and change it to different perspective views.

Num Pad

Look at the upper RH (right hand) corner of the 3D Window. You will see **User Perspective** written in small white letters. This means you are seeing a perspective view of the 3D World. **Perspective** is where all the edges of things appear to point toward a single point on an imaginary horizon. Have a play with the keys. Press the keys in the order below or at random. The idea here is to scramble the view in the window.

Num Pad 7   Top perspective view

Num Pad 5   Top orthographic view

Num Pad 1   Front orthographic view

Num Pad 3   Right orthographic view

Num Pad 4, 6, 8, and 2 Rotates the view

Num Pad 0   Camera view (shows you what the camera sees)

Believe it or not there is a logical sequence in all of this and you will understand it with a little practice.

Also try clicking and holding the MMB and dragging the mouse. That should really mess up the view.

Getting Back to Square One

If (when) you find yourself in a pickle, you have completely messed up or you just don't like what you have made sometimes it's best to start over with a **clean slate**.

The expression "Clean Slate" comes from the time when writing was taught using a slate (small blackboard) and chalk. If you got it wrong you wiped it clean and started over.

Starting over is something you will do time and time again especially when you are learning. It's just part of the deal. You will make something and not be satisfied or it will completely go wrong. Making mistakes and starting again helps you to learn.
Starting Over in Blender is Easy!

To start over, go to the **Info Window Header** and click on **File**. Click on **New**.

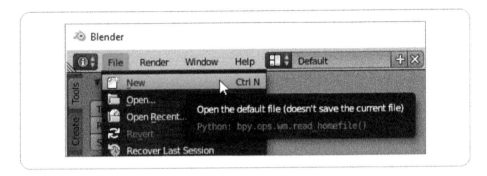

Clicking on **New** reloads the Blender default screen arrangement. A warning message appears saying, **doesn't save the current file.** This means that if you haven't saved your work it will be lost. Don't worry about this just now. I will talk about saving later.

Also when you click **New,** a window appears where you have to click **Reload Start-Up File.** This gives you a second chance to save if you want to.

So far you have only been messing about with messing up the scene so you don't need to save anything. You will learn how to do that later.

For now just click on **Reload Start-Up File** and Blender will do just that, and put the 3D Window back to the way it was when you first started. **You are back to square one.**

I know you are itching to do something so we will make a scene and make an image. In the process I will show you a few more of Blender's features and get you used to following these peculiar instructions. This will be like Shannon flying before he hatched from the egg. We will probably get scrambled. It will also be like playing with fire.

Remember, you can always go back to square one.

Taking a test drive is fun but when you are trying something new there is always a process of trial and error. Sometimes you will lose your way, sometimes you will break down, and sometimes you will crash. Crashing Blender is part of the learning process.

The Properties Window

In demonstrating how to manipulate what you see on the computer screen by rotating the view or moving an Object, you have been working within the 3D Window. This is where you will make models of things and set up scenes and animate the models to move. The 3D Window is the windscreen in front of the driver's seat. The mouse is the steering wheel. The Properties Window is the dashboard containing the buttons and switches for controlling things.

Do not attempt to memorize what all the buttons and switches do. Just like driving a new car for the first time you can get by with a few basics like a pedal to push to make the car go, a pedal to make it stop, and a steering wheel to point it in the right direction. You can worry about the overdrive and headlights and the stereo system later.

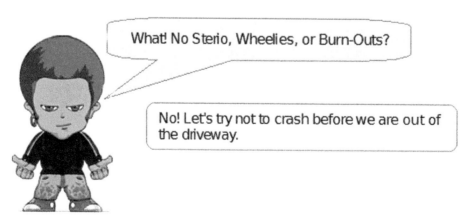

What! No Sterio, Wheelies, or Burn-Outs?

No! Let's try not to crash before we are out of the driveway.

Look at the 12 buttons along the top of the Properties Window. I'm not including the Properties Window icon in the count.

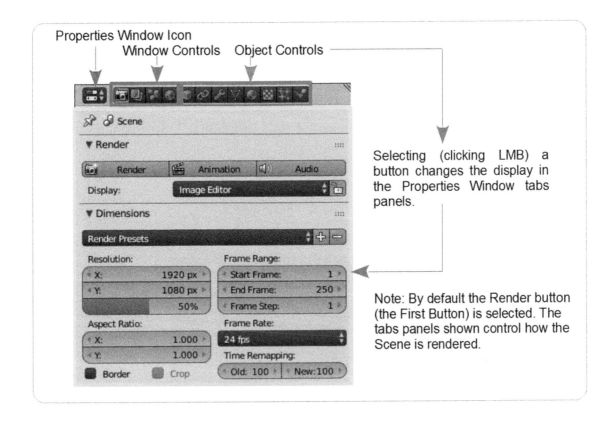

The first four buttons display control tabs with buttons and sliders for adjusting values which control how an image of the scene in the 3D Window or an animation is rendered.

Rendering is the process of converting what you see in the 3D Window into a digital image or movie file.

The remaining eight buttons display control tabs for controlling the properties of an Object that you have selected in the 3D Window. Each Object has its own set of properties. Selecting a different Object displays the properties which have been assigned to the selected Object.

Objects are anything included in the 3D Window Scene. That is, any model you have made or imported, any lamps, and any camera.

Changing Values

As you progress through the examples in the book I will give instructions to change numeric values. Where values are displayed in the Blender interface, they are usually in a panel as shown here in the **Properties Window**.

The Properties Window is at the RHS (right-hand side) of the default Blender screen.

The window displays by default with the **Render buttons** active which is one of 12 button selections available.

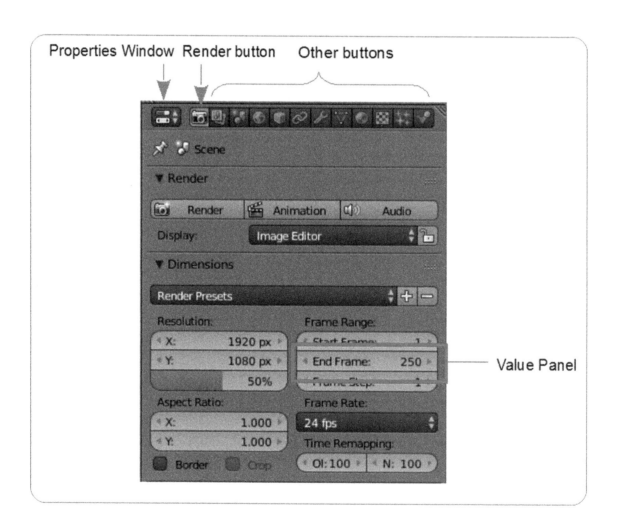

Properties Window   Render button   Other buttons

Value Panel

The Value Panel is a **Slider**, which means you can click LMB in the panel, hold the mouse button down, and drag the mouse left to right to change the value.

Alternatively you may click LMB in the panel (the value shifts to the left of the panel), press delete on your keyboard, and retype a new value. Press Enter.

The two little arrows at either end of the panel allow you to click LMB and incrementally increase or decrease the value.

Chapter 2
Playing With Fire

Playing With Fire

This will be **EXCITING**! I won't explain much about what is going on or why you are doing things. I just want to show you some neat stuff and get you interested. Along the way, I will introduce you to some of the Blender controls.

In the introduction, we looked at the **3D Window** with the **Cube Object** located at the center of the **World**. The Cube Object is one of ten **Primitive** shapes with which you start to make models of all different sorts of things.

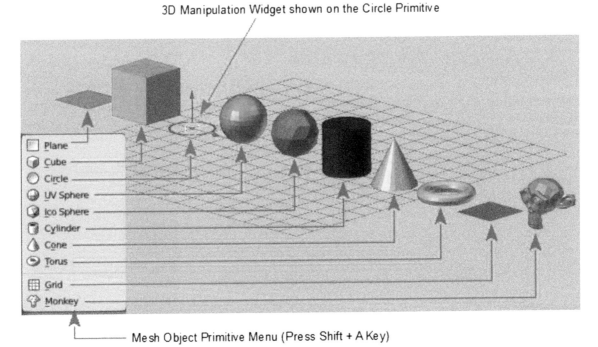

3D Manipulation Widget shown on the Circle Primitive

Mesh Object Primitive Menu (Press Shift + A Key)

The Ten Primitive Shapes

You can join the shapes together and change the shape of the shape to whatever you want. I will explain how to do that later on.

Let's change the **Cube** in the **3D Window** to a different shape. A sphere is a nice shape for demonstrating. You will see in the diagram that there are two sphere types; **UV Sphere** and **Ico Sphere**. We will use the **UV Sphere**.

In the **3D Window** have the **Cube Object** selected (orange outline). Press the **X Key** on the keyboard then click LMB **OK Delete** to remove the cube. To add a sphere into the scene, there are two methods. You will find that there is nearly always more than one way to do something.

How to Add a Sphere

To add a **Sphere Object** click on **Add** in the **3D Window Header** then place the mouse cursor over **Mesh** and click on **UV Sphere** in the selection menu that appears. A UV Sphere will be placed in the 3D Window wherever the 3D Window cursor has been located.

The second method is to press **Shift + A Key** on the keyboard with the mouse cursor in the 3D Window. This opens the same selection menu in the 3D Window. Click on UV Sphere.

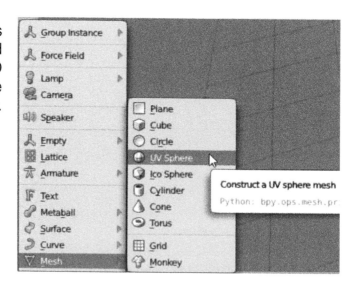

Set the Sphere on Fire

With the sphere selected (orange outline) and the mouse cursor in the **3D Window**, press the **Space Bar** on the keyboard. Pressing the Space Bar opens a **Search Window**. Type "Quick Smoke" in the panel at the top of the Search Window. The single entry Quick Smoke will be in the list below. Click on **Quick Smoke**.

> Quick Smoke is one of BLENDER'S several quick methods.

The 3D Window will change showing the sphere as a **Wire Frame** mesh inside a cuboid.

In the bottom LH (left hand) corner of the 3D Window at the bottom of the **Tool Panel,** you will see Quick Smoke with a **Smoke Style** panel with Smoke inside. Click on the panel and select: **Smoke + Fire.**

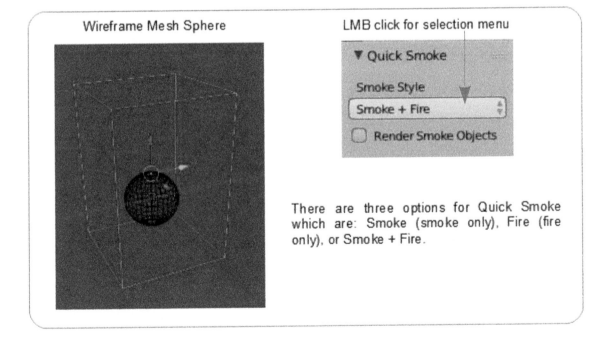

Wireframe Mesh Sphere

LMB click for selection menu

There are three options for Quick Smoke which are: Smoke (smoke only), Fire (fire only), or Smoke + Fire.

This has set Blender to produce a **Simulation** of the sphere burning. The Simulation is an **Animation**. Animations are played in the Timeline Window.

The Timeline Window

The Timeline Window has buttons similar to those on a CD or video player. To see the sphere burning, simply press the Play button. The animation plays for a set time then repeats until you press Stop. Once you have pressed the Play button, it changes to a Stop button.

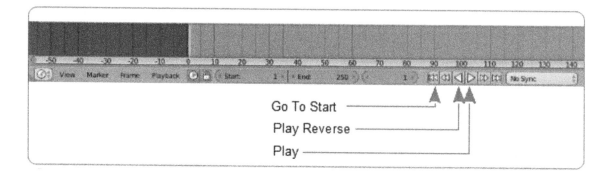

Go To Start

Play Reverse

Play

Press the Stop button somewhere in the middle of the animation to see a still view of the burning Sphere. Press the Go To Start button to start the animation over.

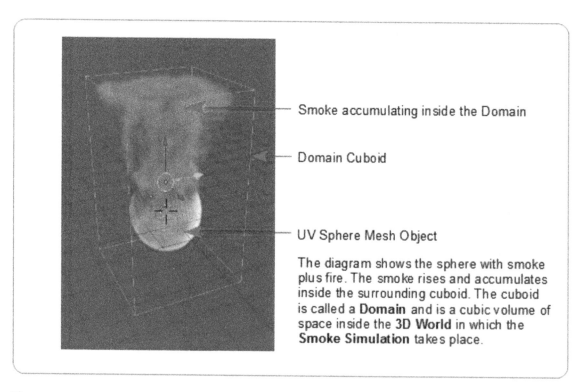

Smoke accumulating inside the Domain

Domain Cuboid

UV Sphere Mesh Object

The diagram shows the sphere with smoke plus fire. The smoke rises and accumulates inside the surrounding cuboid. The cuboid is called a **Domain** and is a cubic volume of space inside the **3D World** in which the **Smoke Simulation** takes place.

There are a lot of settings and controls in the Timeline Window but for now only use the buttons described. Press the Go To Start button, then in the Tool Panel, Quick Smoke tab, select the different Smoke Style options. Play an animation for each option and see the different effects.

This Camp Fire is made using the Quick Smoke method. There is a small cube under the pile of sticks which has Quick Smoke applied.

The rocket is another quick example using Quick Smoke. It has a small UV Sphere on fire placed at the end of a second UV Sphere which has been scaled to form the rocket shape.

Before you can make things and use Quick Smoke to add effects, you have to learn about modeling and applying Materials.

There are lots of different parts to Blender that make different effects. The trick is to understand what each part does, then combine the parts in the correct order for what you want.

To see the UV Sphere burning as an image, press the F12 button on the keyboard. What you see in the 3D Window will be rendered as a digital image.

The 3D Window changes into a different window called the UV Image Editor Window showing the rendered image.

To change back to the 3D Window, press the Esc Key on the keyboard.

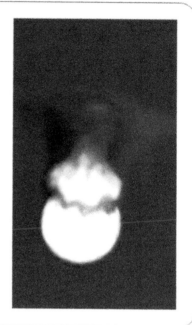

In the example of the Quick Smoke method, a UV Sphere has been used as a model. Remember the sphere is one of ten Primitive shapes in Blender. You may use any of these as well as any model that you make.

As an example work through the following exercise.

Start a new Blender Scene and delete the default Cube. Add a Mesh, Circle Object (press Alt + A Key and select Mesh—Circle). Remember selecting means clicking LMB on the item in the menu.

The Circle Object is entered in the Scene at the location of the 3D Window Cursor. The 3D Window Cursor is the little dotted circle with the cross hairs.

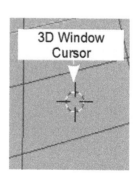

By default this cursor is located at the center of the Scene in the 3D Window but when you click (LMB) anywhere in the 3D Window the cursor gets located at wherever you click.

To put the 3D Window cursor back at the center of the Scene, press **Shift** + **S Key** on the keyboard to bring up the Snap menu, then select **Cursor to Center** from the menu.

When an Object is added to a Scene, it is entered in Object Mode. If you were to use the Quick Smoke method at this time and pressed Play in the Timeline Window, you would be very disappointed to see that there is no smoke or fire.

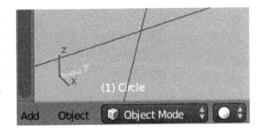

When you entered the Circle Object, you selected **Mesh** then Circle from the menu. You selected a Mesh Object as being a shape made out of something like a fishing net or a piece of chicken coop wire. There are strands of twine or wire joined where they intersect. As an example, look at a UV Sphere Mesh Object.

The image shows a sphere in **Wireframe Display Mode** which illustrates the concept.

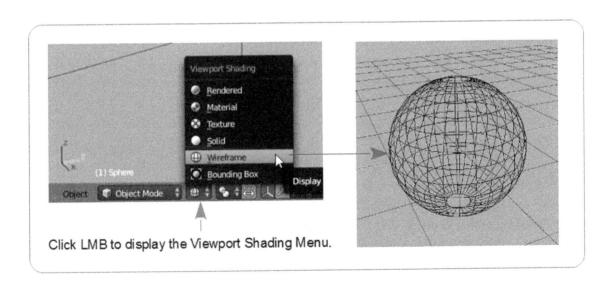

Click LMB to display the Viewport Shading Menu.

Objects in the 3D Window can be viewed in different **Viewport Shading modes.**

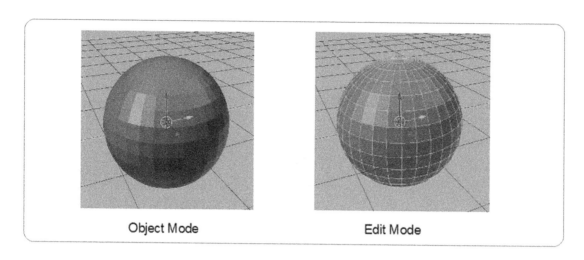

Object Mode   Edit Mode

The UV Sphere in Edit Mode also illustrates the mesh concept.

Let's get back to the Circle Mesh Object.

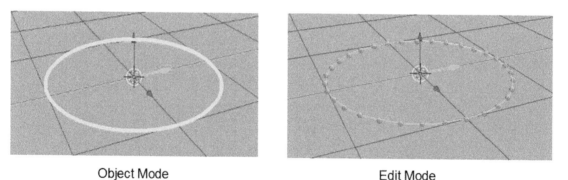

Object Mode   Edit Mode

The circle displays in Object Mode as an orange circle. In Edit Mode, you have the same circle but you also have little orange dots spaced around the circumference. Think of the circle as separate short pieces of wire joined at each end forming a circle. The joints are called **Vertices**. Now, if you tried to set a wire circle on fire, you will have a hard time doing it. On the other hand if you have a piece of wire mesh with some combustible fabric stretched over it, you will be able to set the fabric on fire.

What you have to do is form the circle into a mesh with a surface.

With the circle selected in the 3D Window (orange outline) in **Object Mod**e, press the **Tab Key** to place it in **Edit Mode**. You will have an orange circle with the vertices (dots) all selected. **Get your hand off your mouse**, press the **E Key** (extrude) and press **Enter**. It appears as if nothing has changed but, in fact, you have duplicated a set of vertices which are superimposed over the original set.

Have your mouse cursor positioned in the 3D Window off to one side. Press the **S Key** (scale). The mouse cursor arrow changes to a white cross on top of a black arrow with a broken line connected to the center of the circle. Move the mouse cursor toward the center of the circle. Only move slightly, which moves the duplicated set of

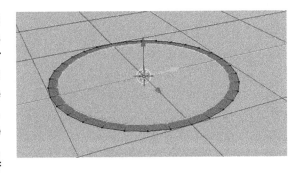

vertices in. You now have an outer and inner set of vertices forming a ring.

The spaces between the vertices are shown gray which indicates that they are filled in or faced. The faces are your fabric. Tab back to Object Mode and apply the Quick Smoke method as you did for the UV Sphere.

Before you apply Quick Smoke, rotate the ring on either the X or Y axis by pressing the **R Key** (rotate) + X or Y and moving your mouse. Place other objects in the scene.

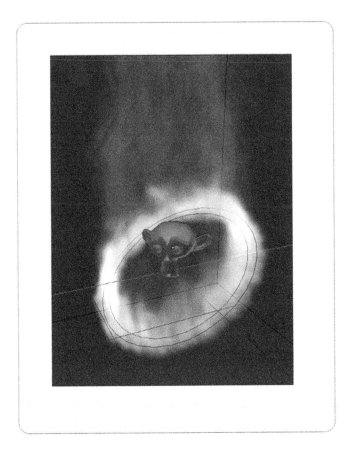

Chapter 3
Quick Explode

Exploding the Quick Way

The previous chapter showing how to set something on fire is one of Blender's quick methods. Exploding also has a **Quick Method.** In a new Blender scene replace the default Cube with a UV Sphere.

Quick Method is fun and easy to use but there is a lot more you can do when you understand the long way.

A plain old gray sphere isn't very exciting so let's give it some color.

This is where the **Properties Window** comes into play. That's the window at the RHS of the screen with a row of buttons in the **Header** at the top and squillions of buttons and sliders and settings going down to the bottom of the screen.

Don't Panic!

Don't Panic!!

Don't Panic!

Don't panic. Just follow along and you will be fine. Remember if the Worst happens you can always go back to **Square One**.

When you first look at the **Properties Window** and you look at the buttons in the **Header**, you see the **Render button** option active. Underneath are the controls for setting how you want a picture or a video to be made.

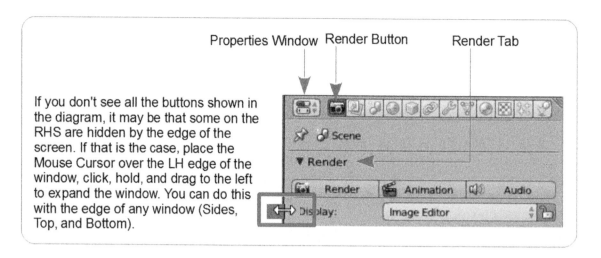

Properties Window   Render Button   Render Tab

If you don't see all the buttons shown in
the diagram, it may be that some on the
RHS are hidden by the edge of the
screen. If that is the case, place the
Mouse Cursor over the LH edge of the
window, click, hold, and drag to the left
to expand the window. You can do this
with the edge of any window (Sides,
Top, and Bottom).

At this point we are not concerned with the Render buttons, instead we want to
select the Material button. For the time being, think of Materials as Color.

As a way of directing you to the various parts of the Properties Window I will adopt the
convention of referring to the Properties Window followed by the Button then a Tab.

For Example: Go to the Properties Window, Render button, and Render tab.

Therefore for Color go to the Properties Window, Material button, click on New.

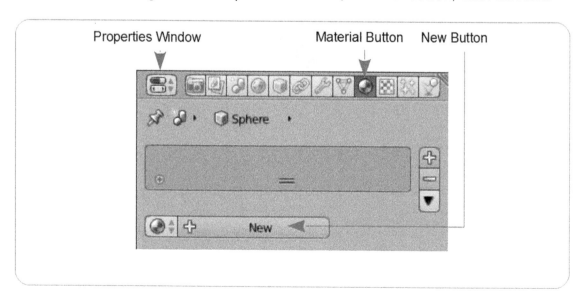

Properties Window   Material Button   New Button

Clicking on **New** will open buttons for controlling the color of the **Object** that you
have selected in the **3D Window**. We have the **UV Sphere** selected so the buttons

will control the color of the sphere. If you had some other Object selected, the buttons would affect that Object.

In Blender, color is controlled by the **Material buttons**. **Color** is only one part of what an **Object** looks like. You can have a red sphere but it can be any shade of red or it could be shiny or dull or it could reflect other colors from other Objects. This is why we refer to an Objects' **Material** rather than its color.

When you click the **New button**, the **Properties Window** expands showing the controls for setting the Material color. To color the UV Sphere, click in the white panel in the **Diffuse tab**. (I will refer to the different panels in the Properties Window as tabs.) A new panel opens with a colored circle shown. Click anywhere in the circle to select a color for the sphere.

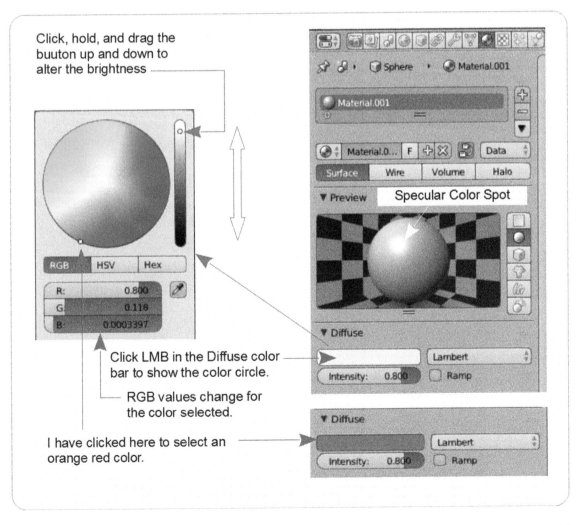

Click, hold, and drag the buuton up and down to alter the brightness

Click LMB in the Diffuse color bar to show the color circle.

RGB values change for the color selected.

I have clicked here to select an orange red color.

The **Diffuse** color is the base color of the Object. The **Specular** color in the tab underneath Diffuse is the color of highlights on a glossy surface. Click in the Specular color bar, select a color, and play with the Intensity slider. You will see the shiny spot on the sphere in the **Preview Window** change.

OK! OK! The Exploding

With our nice colored **UV Sphere** selected in the **3D Window** and the **Mouse cursor** in the window, press the **Space Bar** on the keyboard.

In the Search panel, type **Quick Explode** and select **Quick Explode** from the options.

Ready to go! Press the **Play** button in the **Timeline Window Header.**

Oops! The sphere just fell apart and disappeared off the bottom of the screen. When you press **Stop** in the middle of the animation, you see the broken sphere hanging in space. If you press the **Return to Start** button, you have a cluster of broken bits.

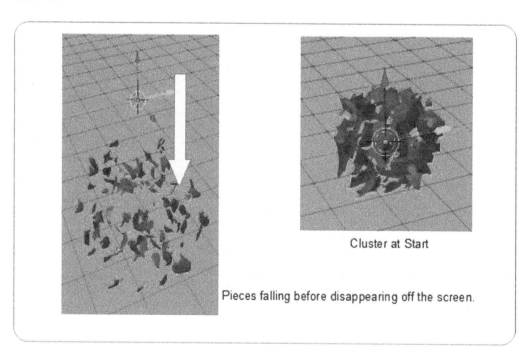

Cluster at Start

Pieces falling before disappearing off the screen.

The sphere breaks into pieces and falls because there is a gravitational force effect applied. You will turn that off in a moment. Look at the lower left of the screen in the **Tools Panel**. You will see **Quick Explode** controls. Each of the gray bars are sliders where you change values. Click, hold, and drag in the **Amount of Pieces** slider bar and make the value approximately 700. Replay the animation and see the difference.

Change the **Outward Velocity** value to 10 and see a real explosion when you replay the animation. Gravity is still in effect but it doesn't have time to do much.

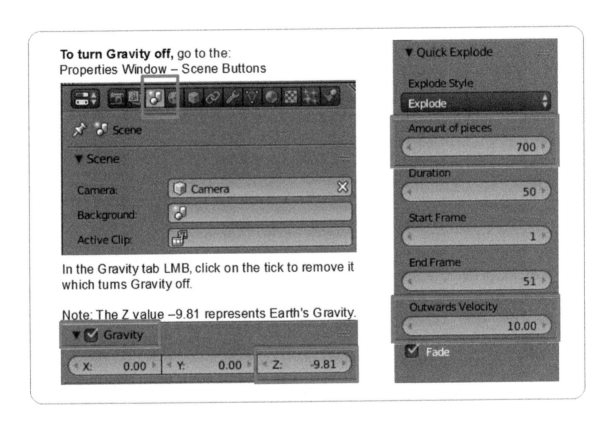

In the **Gravity tab** LMB, click on the tick to remove it which turns Gravity off.

Note: The Z value –9.81 represents Earth's Gravity.

If you return to the **Quick Explode Tool Panel** and reduce the **Outward Velocity** value to something really low like 0.73, when you play the animation the pieces of the sphere float out into space.

BUT HEY! Where do they go?

Look at the **Timeline Window** when you play the animation. A green line moves from left to right. This is the **Timeline Cursor**. Note the numbers along the bottom of the Timeline. These are **Frames** in the animation (like the frames in a piece of old movie film). The green line moves from Frame 1 to Frame 250 then the animation replays. But note the Duration and End Frame values in the Tool Panel. Although the animation in the Timeline is playing for 250 frames, the life of the broken sphere parts lasts only for 50 frames. You can play with these values and see the different effects.

Note: When you change values in the Tools Panel, Gravity reinstates itself so you have to turn it off again.

Look what happens when you have three separate spheres with different colors and different **Outward Velocity** values.

All spheres are located in the same space at the center of the scene, but when they explode the parts fly apart at different speeds and you see the different colors.

A rendered image of the Scene is not very spectacular.

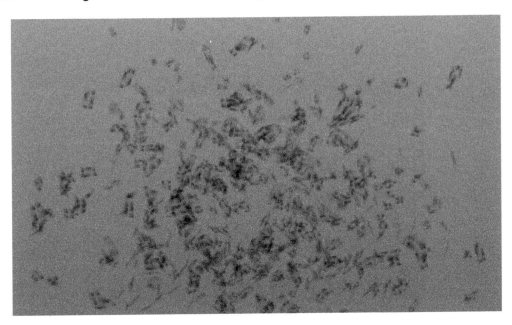

A second render with a simple tweak is much more spectacular.

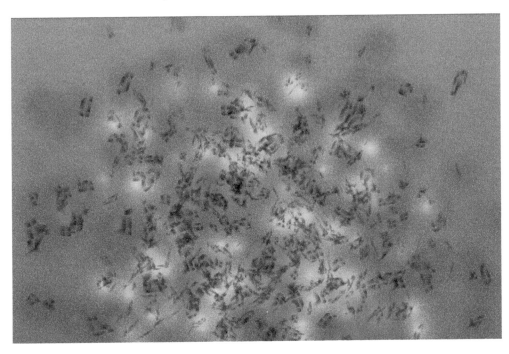

To produce these renders, it will be better if you take the long road and understand a little more about the BLENDER controls.

Chapter 4
Exploding the Long Way

Exploding the Long Way

Using the quick method to explode in Blender is easy and fun but taking the long way round teaches you even more cool stuff. You can still start with the same UV Sphere and give it a **Material** (color) but then you apply a **Particle System** and a **Modifier**.

A Particle System makes an object throw off little dots which show as fuzzy points of light when you make a picture. Sort of like fuzzy stars. You can control how the Particles fly and move and make them look like other things.

When you use **Particles** for exploding a sphere, you make the broken bits of the sphere follow the particles.

A Modifier is a prearranged piece of computer code which makes something happen. Don't worry you don't have to be a coder nor understand the code, you just have to know which buttons to press.

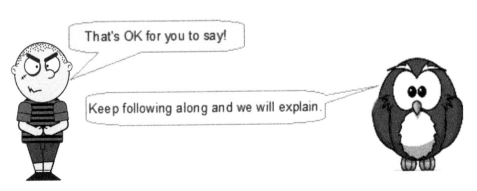

Let's Make a Particle System

Have your **UV Sphere** selected in the **3D Window** then go over and look at the **Properties Window Header**. Find the **Particles button**.

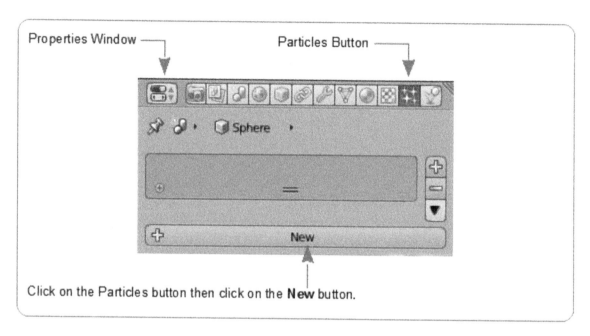

Properties Window

Particles Button

Sphere

New

Click on the Particles button then click on the **New** button.

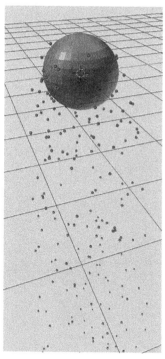

Yes! There are more buttons and panels and sliders and controls.

Blender is a very powerful tool that can make fantastic effects. To drive it is like flying a jumbo jet. There are lots and lots of switches in the cockpit. No one learns to fly an airplane in 5 minutes and they never start off in a jumbo.

With all the buttons showing you have applied a **Particle System** to the **UV Sphere** and this has automatically set up an animation. Look in the **Timeline Window** and you will see a faint red line across the bottom. This shows that an animation sequence is in place.

Remember Gravity! That is also working.

Press **Play** in the **Timeline Window Header**.

Particles are emitted from the surface of the sphere and fall under the effect of Gravity. The Particles continue to be emitted until just before the end of the animation sequence in the Timeline.

You can click the **Stop** button and then the **Go To Start** button.

Click, hold, and drag the green **Timeline Window Cursor** to the right to see the particles at different positions in the animation.

Turn Gravity off and replay (Properties Window, Scene buttons, Gravity tab).

This time the **Particles** float off into space but they only stay in view for 50 frames. If you look in the **Properties Window, Particles buttons, Emission tab**, you will see a Lifetime value: 50.000. If you increase this value (click, hold, and drag in the panel), the Particles will remain visible longer.

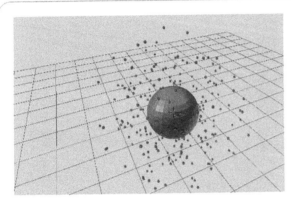

Particles at 50 Frames

Note: I have cheated. Just a little bit. I have made the particles display as tiny spheres. This is something you can do in Blender. Your particles will be tiny orange dots which do not show too well in an image.

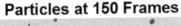
Particles at 150 Frames

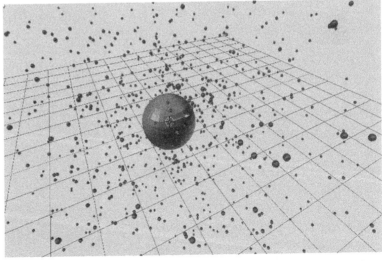

To give you a taste of how you can control the particles go to the start at Frame 1 then in the **Properties Window, Particle buttons, Velocity tab,** and change the **Emitter Object: Y** value to 10. This gives the particles a start speed in the Y direction when they are emitted so they shoot off along the Y axis in the scene.

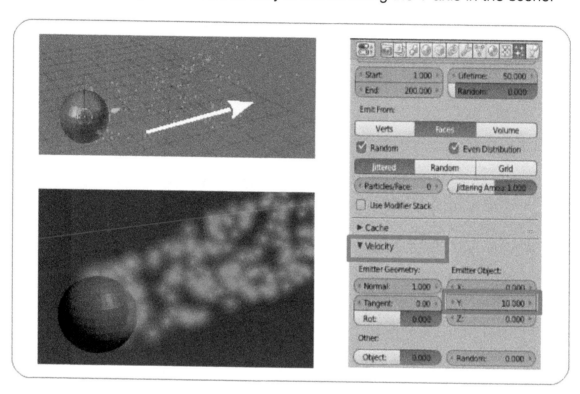

When you **Render** (Press F12) and make the **Camera View** in the **3D Window** into a picture, you see the **Particles** as fuzzy points of light. They are the same color as the Sphere's Material.

Let's Blow It Up

To blow the sphere up (make it fly apart), we add an **Explode Modifier**.

You must have the Particle System in place first.

In the **Properties Window Header**, click on the **Modifier button.**

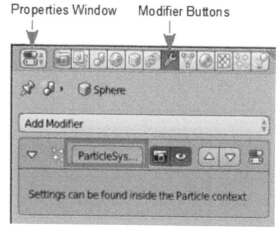

You will see that there is a Modifier already applied which is the Particle System. Click on the **Add Modifier** button and in the selection menu that displays under **Simulate**, click on **Explode**.

The Explode Modifier is added to the Modifier Stack (Modifiers are stacked one on top of the other in the Properties Window).

In the **Timeline Window**, play the animation again and see the sphere disintegrate with parts flying off in the same direction as the particles.

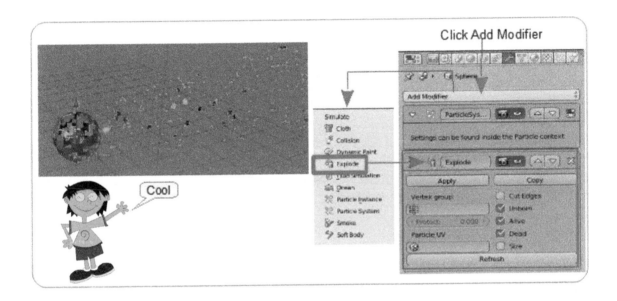

Render an image (press F12).

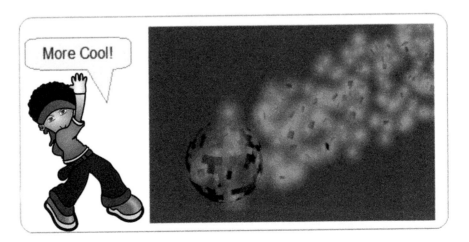

Exploding a Different Way

There are always more ways than one to do something depending on the effect that you want. We will make a simple fireworks type of explosion.

Start a new Blender scene and replace the default **Cube** with a **UV Sphere**.

Scale the sphere down. To do this precisely so that you get the same results that I will show you, press the N Key on your keyboard to display the **Object Properties** panel at the RHS of the 3D Window.

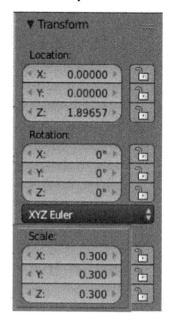

Remember, the properties in the panel are for the **Object** that is selected in the **3D Window**. In this case, the Object is the **UV Sphere**.

With the mouse cursor in the 3D Window, press the S Key (Scale) and move the cursor toward the sphere. You will see the scale values in the Object Properties panel change as you move the mouse. Move the mouse until the X, Y, and Z values equal 0.30, then click LMB to set the value.

Change the 3D Window to **Camera View** (press Num Pad 0). Click LMB on the blue handle of the **Manipulation Widget** (blue arrow, vertical Z axis), hold, and drag the sphere to the top of the Camera viewport.

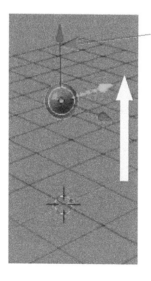

Click LMB, hold and drag up.

In the **Properties Window, Material buttons**, click on the **New button** to apply a material to the sphere. Blender will apply the default gray Material (color). This is fine for the moment but also by default the **Material Type** is set as **Surface**. This is defining how the object is rendered when an image is created. Change this to type **Halo** by simply clicking the Halo button.

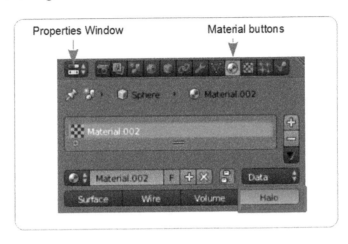

The UV Sphere in the 3D Window changes from a solid sphere to a sphere made up of a group of orange dots.

You can see the different render effects by clicking on each option (Surface, Wire, Volume, Halo) and pressing F12 to render an image with the different options. Remember, press Esc to cancel the rendered view.

Another way? Yes, there is always another way.

Up until now we have been seeing things in the 3D Window in **Solid Viewport Shading mode**. There are other options.

In the 3D Window header, next to Object Mode is the **Viewport Shading options** button (selection menu). You may select the different options and see the different ways things display in the 3D Window. In later versions of Blender, there is the **Rendered option** which puts the 3D Window into **Render mode** letting you see how the Scene will look when rendered. The same as pressing F12 on the keyboard.

To see the different **Material Render** effects, have the 3D Window in Rendered Viewport Shading mode and select the different Material Render options in turn.

In our case, with the **Material Render, Halo option** selected, the sphere displays in the 3D Window as a group of orange dots when in **Solid Viewport Shading mode.** In **Rendered Viewport Shading mode**, it displays as a fuzzy ball of white light.

The sphere displays as a group of orange dots.

The dots are the vertices of the surface mesh.

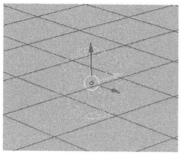

Solid Viewport Shading   Rendered Viewport Shading

The orange dots are actually the vertices of the mesh surface of the sphere. The Material Render, Halo option says, displays the vertices as little points of light so the group of orange dots looks like a ball of light when rendered.

If you change the Material color of the UV Sphere, the dots will display as whatever color you select and the ball of light will be that color.

Note: With the material Halo option selected, the Properties Window, Materials buttons have changed. There is a Halo tab with controls for affecting the halo display, one of which is a color bar for selecting the Diffuse Material color.

Change Back to Solid Viewport Shading Mode

With Material, Render, Halo, click in the color bar to change the Diffuse Material color.

We are off the track a little when it comes to Exploding but believe me, it is connected.

In the previous example of exploding we saw how the surface of the UV Sphere flew apart following Particles. We will do the same thing this time but now the vertices showing as little points of light will follow the Particles.

The UV Sphere is still selected in the 3D Window. In the Properties Window add a Particle System.

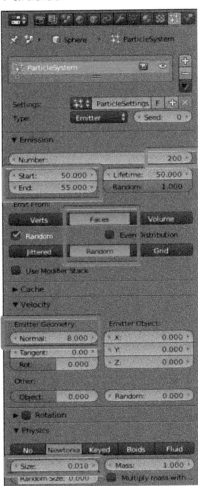

Change the values as shown in the diagram. The main points in these settings are, we are making the particles emit in a random order, and that by setting the Start Frame to 50 and the End Frame to 55, the explosion takes place during five frames of the animation (at 24 Frames per second that is 0.208 seconds).

If you play the animation with the 3D Window in Rendered Viewport Shading mode, at best nothing will happen or at worst the program will crash. The computer just cannot process the information in the time. Well, mine can't.

Change back to Solid Viewport Shading, play the animation then move the Timeline Window cursor somewhere past Frame 55 and render an image (F12) or put the 3D Window in Rendered Viewport Shading mode.

Repositioning the Timeline Window cursor will cause the 3D Window to re-render.

You can add multiple spheres to the scene and experiment with different particle settings to create a real fireworks display.

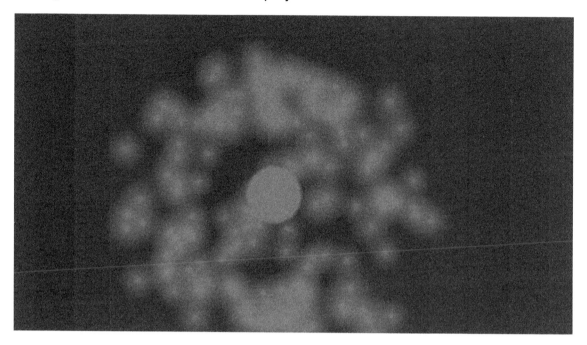

Rendered Image at Frame 60

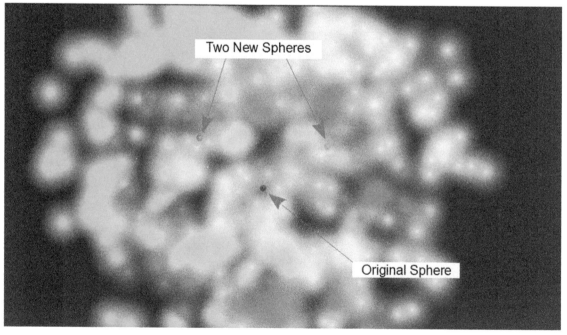

Rendered Image with Two Spheres Added with Different Materials

Chapter 5
Modeling

Modeling

The question you have been asking all along is, "How do I make something?"

Here goes! You will have to follow carefully and sorry, but I will have to take you back to Moving About and expand on the subject. Sometimes there is no getting away with shortcuts.

Start a new Blender scene.

Orange Outline

You will have the default screen arrangement with the gray **Cube Object** at the center.

Zoom in a little (scroll the mouse wheel if you have one or press Num Pad plus +).

The cube is selected as shown by its orange outline. When in this state, it is said to be in **Object Mode**. You see this in the **3D Window Header**.

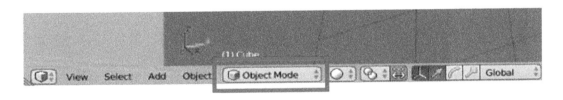

In **Object Mode**, you see the outer surfaces of the cube with a gray **Material** applied. The default **Cube Object** is the only object that has a material pre-applied. When you enter other objects into a scene, you have to manually apply a **Material** (new objects display as the defauly gray but the Material is not applied).

At the beginning of the book, in the introduction, I briefly talked about moving objects. This was mainly how to move in a straight line and how to rotate the scene in the 3D Window. Remember this diagram?

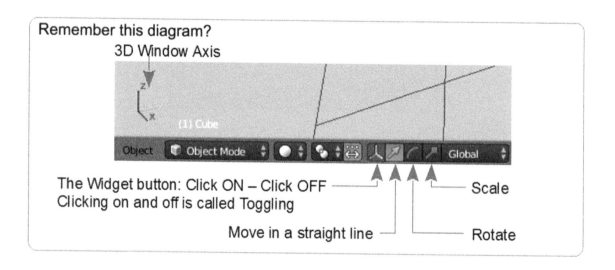

I said that you move an **Object** in a straight line by using the **Manipulation Widget** or by pressing the **G Key** and grabbing the Object. Since this is Blender there are more options. To demonstrate I will use the default **Cube Object** as a starter.

Moving Straight Line ..... Click on a Widget arrow and drag the mouse.

Press the G Key + X, Y, or Z and drag the mouse.

Moving Freely................. Press the G Key, hold, and drag the mouse.

Rotating .... Change the Widget to rotation mode. Click on one of the rotation handles (circles) and drag the mouse.

Press the R Key + X, Y, or Z to rotate about an axis.

Scaling........................... Change the Widget to scale mode. Click on one of the handles and move the mouse away or toward the object.

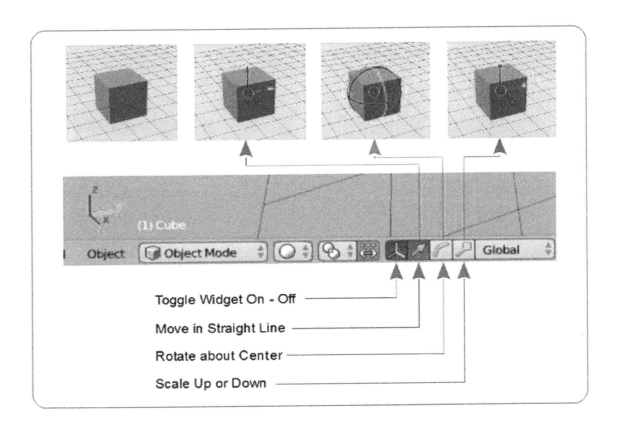

Toggle Widget On - Off ────────────

Move in Straight Line ────────────

Rotate about Center ────────────

Scale Up or Down ────────────

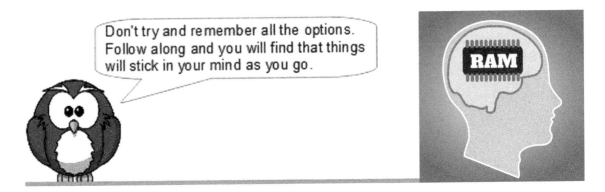

Don't try and remember all the options.
Follow along and you will find that things
will stick in your mind as you go.

RAM

OK! Now you know how to move an **Object** and scale it. To model something in Blender, you start with any of the **Primitive** shapes that are available (press Shift + A for the selection menu).

Once you have selected a shape, you then modify (change) the shape.

To change a shape, you place the **Object** in **Edit Mode**. To do this, have the object selected, then simply press the **Tab Key**.

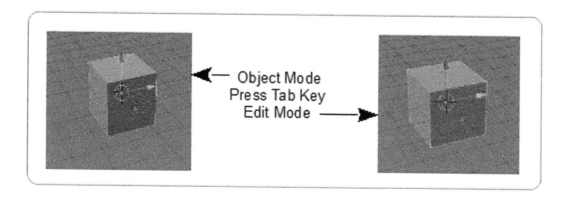

You can also change modes in the **3D Window Header** but since you will be changing modes frequently it is much more convenient to press the **Tab Key**.

Look at the **Cube Object** in **Edit Mode**. What you see is the cube with little orange dots at the corners and orange edges. The dots are called **Vertices** and since they are all orange in color they are selected.

Press the A Key to deselect and press the A Key again to select. This procedure of pressing a key to select and deselect is called **Toggling**. Toggle to deselect the vertices.

In **Edit Mode**, you can select (click RMB) a single vertex and move it to reshape a **Primitive**.

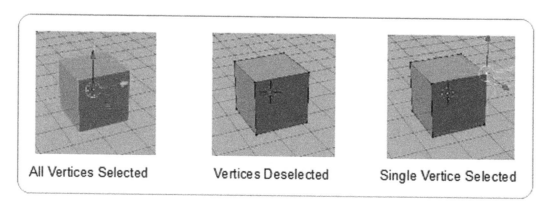

All Vertices Selected   Vertices Deselected   Single Vertice Selected

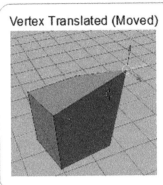

Vertex Translated (Moved)

Move vertices by clicking RMB to select and use the Manipulation Widget or by clicking RMB, then the G Key (Grab), and moving the mouse.

The cube is OK as a starting point to explain the very basics of shaping by moving vertices, but I must admit it is not very exciting. There is only one Primitive in Blender that is anywhere near being complex which will show you how an object is constructed.

Meet Suzanne

Suzanne is a Monkey Object.

Suzanne – Object Mode

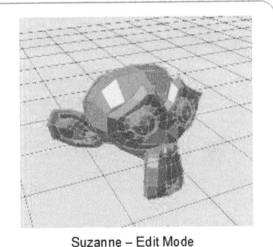

Suzanne – Edit Mode

No kidding!

You find Suzanne in with all the other Primitives.

That's no reflection on Suzanne. It's not nice to call her primitive just because you think you are so clever.

When you select Suzanne, she will show up on the screen as a plain old gray monkey looking to the left. The other way round.

I have given her a Material (color) and rotated her for a better look at her beautiful face.

Oh Yes! I have also changed the background color. I will show you how later.

You can deselect **Suzanne's** vertices while she is in **Edit Mode**, then select a single vertex or even a group of vertices and move them about to make her even more beautiful. You select more than one vertex by holding the Shift Key while clicking RMB. If you have the **Manipulation Widget** turned on, the Widget locates to the center of the **Vertex Group**. You can use it to move the vertices.

Selecting vertices is only one way of changing the shape of an Object.

Look at the **3D Window Header** while you are in **Edit Mode**.

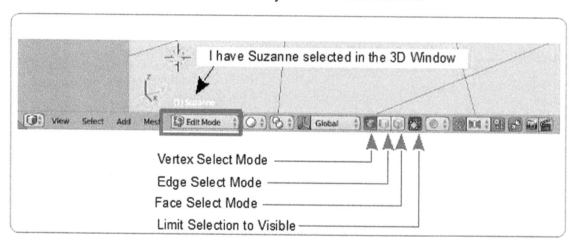

Besides selecting Vertices, you can select Edges or Faces by changing the selection mode.

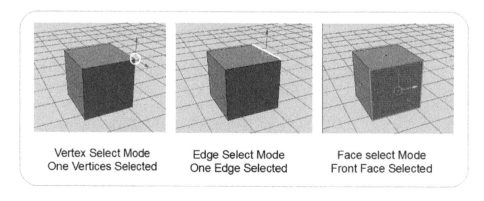

| Vertex Select Mode | Edge Select Mode | Face select Mode |
| One Vertices Selected | One Edge Selected | Front Face Selected |

The **Limit Selection to Visible** button toggles between, allowing you to select only the vertex, edge, or face that you see on the screen (the front of an object) or vertices, edges, and faces that are on the back of an object.

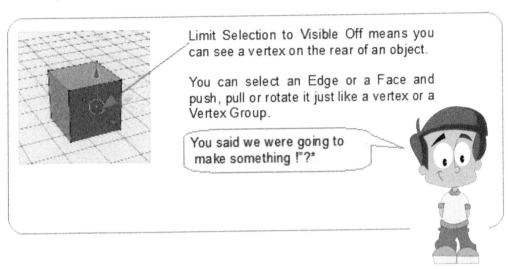

Limit Selection to Visible Off means you can see a vertex on the rear of an object.

You can select an Edge or a Face and push, pull or rotate it just like a vertex or a Vertex Group.

You said we were going to make something !"?*

OK! OK! We will but first there is one more thing.

You will have to know how to **Extrude**.

Extrusion means taking a shape and stretching it out to form a different shape. A little while ago I translated a vertex to change the shape of a cube. When you extrude, you duplicate the selected vertices and reposition them to alter a shape.

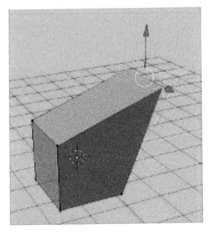

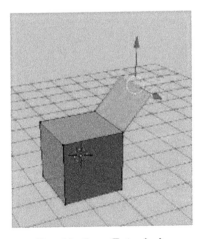

Two Vertices Selected and Translated

Two Vertices Extruded

To **Extrude**, select the vertices, edges, or faces. Press the E Key (Extrude). Drag the mouse and click when in position.

We are ready to go and make something. OK? We will make an aircraft.

Open a new Blender scene. Delete the default Cube and add a UV Sphere. Zoom in (scroll MMB or Num Pad +). Scale down on the Z axis (S Key + Z Key, drag the mouse toward the center of the sphere) as shown in the diagram.

Don't make the pancake too thin.

When you open Blender, the **3D Window** is shown on **User Perspective view**. Look in the top LH corner of the window and you will see User Perspective. Change to **Top Orthographic view**.

Yes it's all a bit confusing but just keep on following along.

To change views, have the **Mouse Cursor** in the **3D Window** and press Num Pad 7. What you get is **Top Perspective view**. The give-away is the line radiating from the **Lamp** toward the flattened sphere.

The Lamp???? Look for a black dot with two dotted circles. That's the Lamp. Also look in the top LH corner of the window to see **Top Perspective**.

You want **Top Orthographic** so press Num Pad 5. Notice the line radiating from the Lamp disappears since you are now looking straight down on the sphere.

Scale the sphere times 2 on the Y axis (Press S key + Y Key + 2 and LMB click).

You will be modeling the reshaped sphere and want it to be identical either side of the Y axis (the green line). That is to say you want it to be mirrored on the X axis (along the red line).

To mirror something place the sphere in **Edit Mode** and delete all the vertices on the LHS (left-hand side) of the Y axis (press the B Key for Box select, place the cursor as shown by the yellow cross, click and hold dragging a rectangle around the LHS vertices). **Don't forget to turn Limit Selection to Visible off**. With the vertices selected, press the X Key and select **Vertices to Delete**. Place the UV Sphere in Object Mode (press Tab).

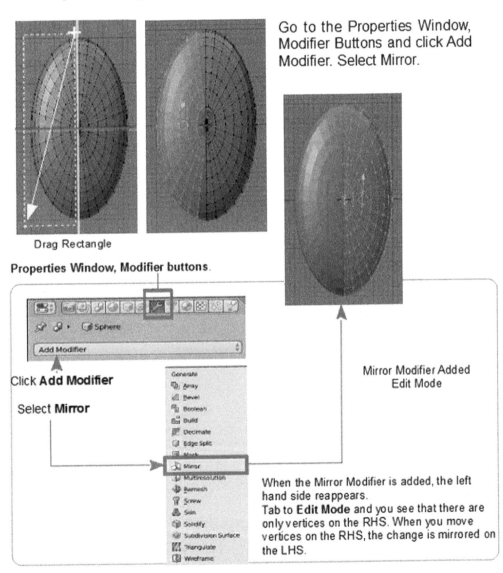

Drag Rectangle

Go to the Properties Window, Modifier Buttons and click Add Modifier. Select Mirror.

Properties Window, Modifier buttons.

Click **Add Modifier**

Select **Mirror**

Mirror Modifier Added
Edit Mode

When the Mirror Modifier is added, the left hand side reappears.
Tab to **Edit Mode** and you see that there are only vertices on the RHS. When you move vertices on the RHS, the change is mirrored on the LHS.

OK! What have we got? A long skinny pancake!

To continue, change the window to **Right Orthographic** view (press the Num Pad 3 Key).

Select the vertices as shown in the diagram (hold Shift and click RMB on each vertex).

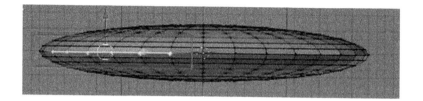

Press Num Pad 7 to change back to **Top Orthographic** view. Press the E Key (Extrude) and use the **Widget** to move the vertices to the right.

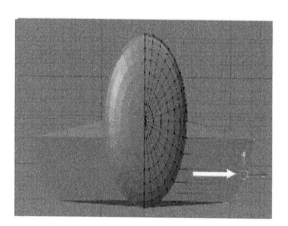

Group Extruded to the Right

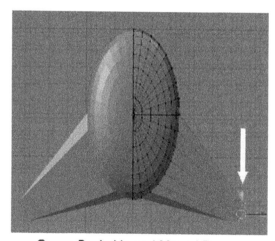

Group Scaled in and Moved Down

With the **Vertex Group** still selected, press the S Key (scale) and scale the group in. Use the **Widget** to move the group down toward the back of the aircraft.

Change to **Front Orthographic** view (Press Num Pad 1). The **Vertex Group** remains selected. Press the E Key (Extrude) and move the extrusion up, then scale in (S Key, drag mouse toward the group). Finally use the Manipulation Widget to move the group back slightly.

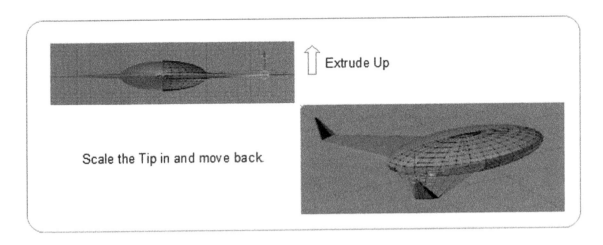

Extrude Up

Scale the Tip in and move back

Keep going you are nearly there.

Select a line of vertices on the center as shown and extrude up.

Scale the group in and move back.

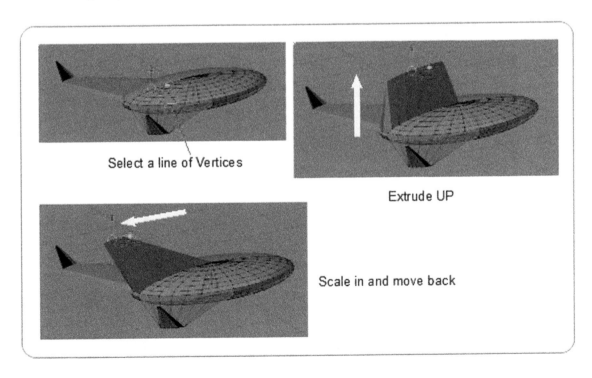

Select a line of Vertices

Extrude UP

Scale in and move back

Go into **Object Mode**, add a **Material**. In the **Tool Panel** at the LHS of the **3D Window** click on the **Smooth** button. Rotate the 3D Window to see your super duper aircraft.

Just a cotton picking minute! How do you get the background looking like sky? You said you would show us how!

Oops sorry! I did, didn't I.

You have your aircraft model finished and placed in the 3D Window the way you want it, like this for instance.

Oh! By the way, I have changed the 3D Window background color to this pale green.

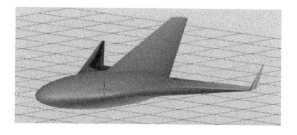

OK! How do you do that?

Changing the 3D Window background color is just one of many things you can change to suit your personal preferences. Guess what? There's a **User Preferences Window** for doing it. Click on the **3D Window icon** in the lower left of the window and select **User Preferences**.

The 3D Window changes to the User Preferences Window.

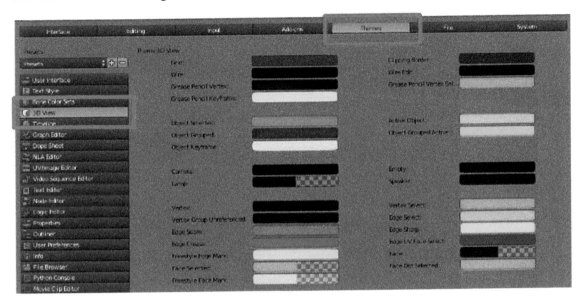

Wow! There are a lot of things to mess with here. Look at the top of this window and click on **Themes** (if it isn't highlighted blue). Now look at the list at the left of the window with all the different window types. Click on **3D View**.

With 3D View selected (highlighted blue) what you see is a whole bunch of colored panels (as shown above) which, when clicked, open color selection circles for the different parts of the 3D Window. You want the 3D Window background. You can look all you want but you won't find it. This is one of Blender's peculiarities. To change the 3D Window background color, you click on the **Gradient High/Off** panel at the lower RHS of the window. In the color circle that displays, you can select a color and adjust the brightness with the vertical slider at the RHS of the panel.

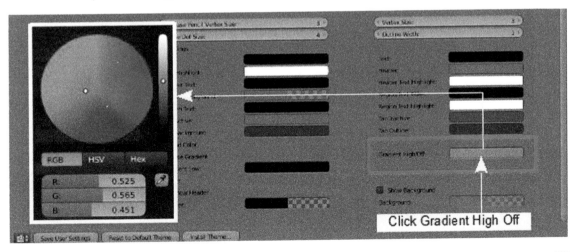

Click Gradient High Off

When you have the color you like, you click **Save User Settings** at the bottom left of the window. Click on the icon in the corner and go back to the 3D Window.

A better way of opening the User Preferences Window is to click on File in the 3D Window header, then select User Preferences from the menu. When you do it this way, the User Preferences Window opens at a reduced size on top of the 3D Window so, when you change the color, you see it happening as you make the change.

Wowsers! There's a lot of stuff.

Well..... You did ask.

Changing the 3D Window background color **will not color the background** of a rendered image. To do this you use the background settings in the **Properties Window, World buttons**. You will have to experiment with these to discover all the options but to get you started look at the **Preview tab** and the **World tab**.

In the **World tab** click on the **Horizon** Color bar and select a blue sky color in the color circle. Use the slider to adjust the brightness. You see the color in the Preview tab panel. Check (tick) **Blend Sky** to add a shading gradient.

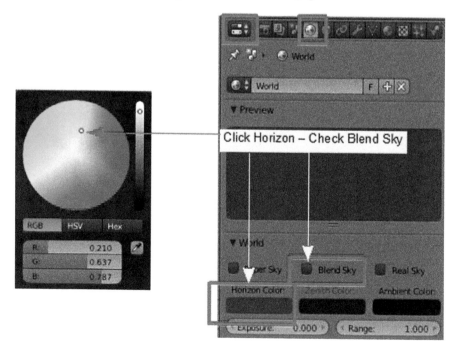

The Properties Window, World buttons will show a preview.

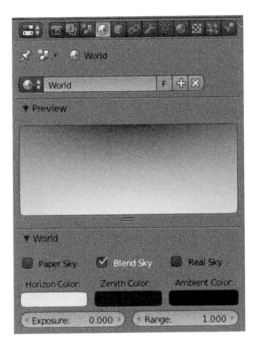

Render an image (F12) to see the image background.

Experiment with the color bars and the Sky settings to see the differences.

A better way. Yes! A better way (there's always a different way) is to use an **Image Textures**. You will have to wait until you learn about Textures before you can use this method. The image below gives you the idea.

Chapter 6
Saving Your Work

Saving Work

Saving something like a model in Blender is simply saving the Blender file in which you made it. Blender files have a **.blend** file extension. That's the bit you put on the end of the **File Name**.

For example: If I want to save a file in which I have made onions, I would name the file:

My_Onions.blend

Now! If you have made some models of onions in a new Blender scene, that is to say, if you have started Blender, deleted the Cube object, and modeled some onions. What you have done is modified the default Blender file. To save the modified file, go to the Info Window Header, click on File then click on **Save** and.......**WHAT HAS HAPPENED?** The Screen changes from the 3D Window to the **File Browser Window**. I will take a little diversion to explain.

Windows

In Blender the default Screen arrangement has five windows open. There are actually 16 different windows listed under **Editor Types**. In the 3D Window Header, click on the icon in the bottom LH corner and you will see the list.

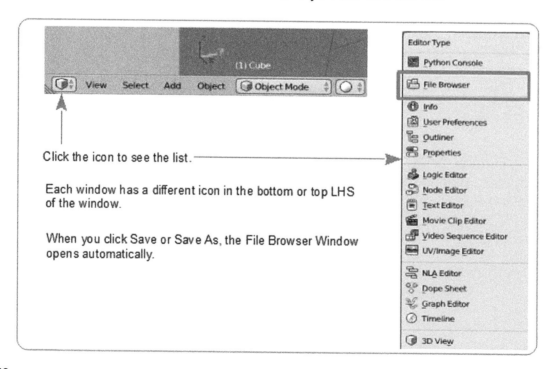

Try this as an experiment. Click the icon at the bottom of the 3D Window and then click on Properties in the list. You will have opened the Properties Window. The original Properties Window remains open at the RHS of the screen. The new window looks different because it is spread across the area that was the 3D Window but you will see the same row of buttons in the top LH corner.

Next to the buttons you see the icon for the Properties Window. Click the icon and select the 3D View from the list. The 3D Window is reinstated.

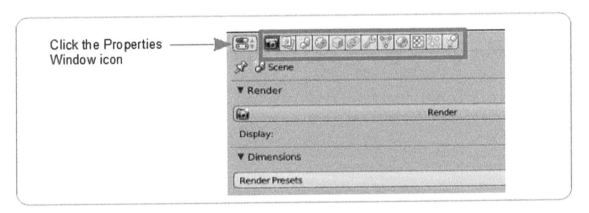

Click the Properties Window icon

I have already mentioned that you can drag the edge of a window but you can also split a window. Splitting divides the window into two identical windows. You can then change one part to a different type. To divide a window, click

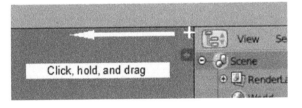

Click, hold, and drag

on the cross hatching in the top right or bottom left of a window (the mouse cursor turns into a white cross), hold, and drag the mouse.

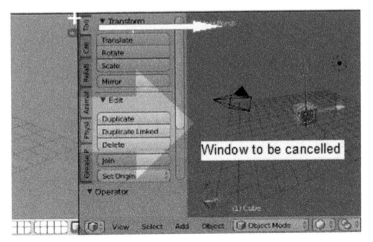

Window to be cancelled

To cancel a window click, hold, and drag the cross into the window to be cancelled. You will see a large arrow pointing into the window.

We haven't finished with saving, so we had better get back to it.

Back to Saving

OK! You clicked on **Save** and the window changed to the **File Browser Window**.

The File Browser Window shows you all the Directories, Folders, and Files saved on the Hard Drive in your computer. Clicking Save opens the window at the last place where you saved something and Blender automatically names your new file untitled.blend. You see the name in the red strip at the top of the window. You can click in the red strip, delete this name, and type your own name. It's preferable to name your file something that you will remember otherwise you are never going to find it again. When you have typed your file name, press Enter. The red strip turns gray. To save your file, click Save Blender File in the top RH corner of the window. You will be taken back to the 3D Window.

Hold on a minute!

I said that the File Browser Window opened at the last place that you previously saved something. Is this where you want to save the new file? Maybe not!

This is where you have to know a bit about navigation. Go get the GPS from the car.

Sorry! GPS isn't going to help. Neither will a compass, a sextant, nor a street map. We will have to take a look at the **File Tree**.

Are we going outside for some fresh air? Is a File Tree anything like a Monkey tree?

No! The File Tree is the way folders and files are arranged on your computer.

It would be good if you understand how files are arranged so that you can save your work and then be able to find a file in the future.

The File Tree

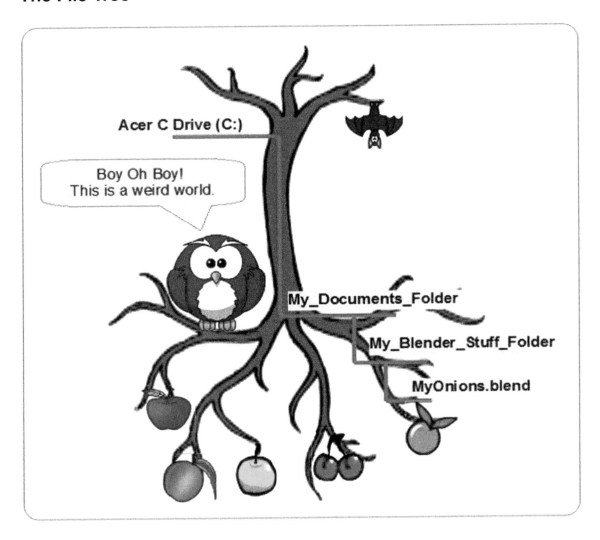

Shannon the Owl is very confused because his world has gone topsy turvy (upside-down). Actually only the File Tree is upside down (Roots at the top, Branches at the bottom).

Roots have nothing to do with the Root Drive on your computer. That's something else, but the main trunk of the tree represents the C: Drive. The Hard Drive on your computer is a disc where all your folders and files and programs are stored. The Hard Drive is divided into partitions which are called Drives and the Drives are named C, D, E, F, etc. The C: Drive is where all your folders and programs are kept. Look at the C: Drive (the tree trunk). There is a branch on the trunk named My_Documents_Folder. (*Note*: I have made these names up so I can explain.) Inside the folder is a subfolder (a smaller branch) named My_Blender_Stuff_Folder and inside this folder is a file (a twig on the small branch) named MyOnions.blend.

You will see this arrangement on a Windows Operating System in Windows Explorer or File Explorer. These are Windows programs that let you see the File Arrangement.

The File Tree: File Explore (Window 10)

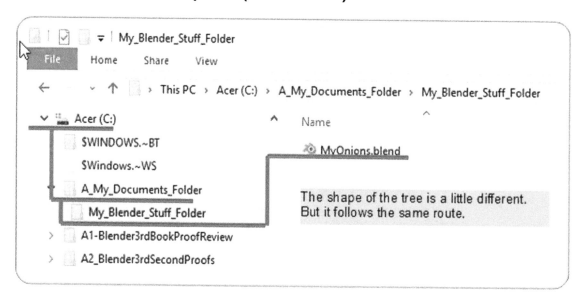

The File Tree: Blender File Browser

In Blender you navigate the File Tree using the File Browser Window. The window opens in stages. When you click Save to save work, the File Browser Window opens, showing the place where you last saved something. This may not be where you want to save something new. To get back to the beginning of the C: Drive, click on the drive in the System tab. The folders in the C: Drive will be listed in the main window panel at the right.

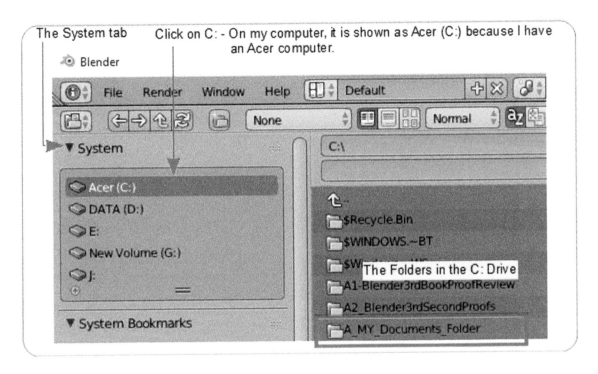

Click on C: - On my computer, it is shown as Acer (C:) because I have an Acer computer.

In the folder list, in the main window panel, you will see the folder named A_My_Documents_Folder. Click LMB on the name to open this folder. You will see the subfolder named My_Blender_Stuff_Folder.

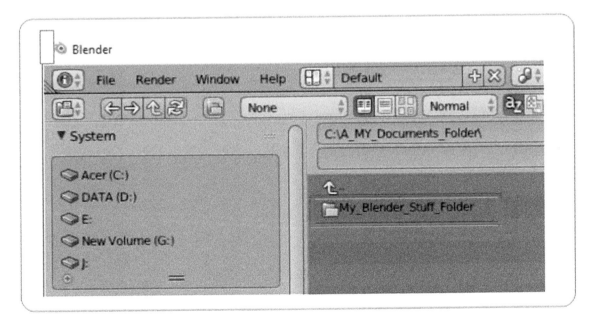

Click on the folder name and inside the folder is the file MyOnions.blend.

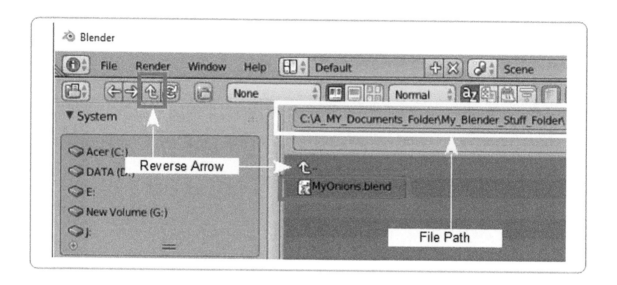

You see the complete File Path in the panel at the top of the main File Browser Window panel.

To navigate back through the File Path, click on either of the reverse arrows.

There are plenty of other options in the File Browser Window but that should do for now.

Go back and remake the model of the super duper aircraft and save a Blender file.

Save or Save As

When you open Blender, you open the default Blender Scene with the Default Cube in the center. You can then model something using the cube or add one or more primitives to construct a model or create a scene. At any time in the process, you can and should save the file. When a model or scene includes a considerable amount of work, you don't want to lose it should your computer crash or the power goes off. **Save your work regularly.**

To recap, you go to the **Info Window** header, click **File** then when you click **Save** the **File**, the **Browser Window** opens. Navigate to where you want to save. Enter a name for your file and click **Save Blender File.**

The next time you start Blender you get the default arrangement again.

To retrieve your work, you go to the **Info Window** header, click **File**, then click **Open**. The **File Browser Window** opens where you navigate to the file that you saved, click on it to select, then click **Open Blender File** in the upper right of the screen.

You can proceed to make changes to the file by adding more models, changing the scenery, etc.

At this point, you may want to save the new work in which case you simply use the **Save** option.

You may want to save the new work but retain what you had before you made the changes. This is where you select the **Save As** option. The **File Browser Window** again opens where you enter a new file name then click **Save Blender File.** This creates a new file with the new name and your original file remains unaltered.

Chapter 7
Materials

In Blender, think of Materials as color and how a color is applied to the surface of an Object. The Object could be the aircraft that you have modeled.

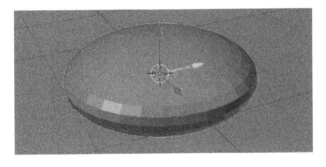

We started by adding a UV Sphere Object into the Scene, squishing down on the Z Axis and extruding bits to form the shape of an aircraft.

The UV Sphere displayed on the screen as a dull gray color. This is the default Blender color, the same as that applied to the default Cube.

Default, according to the dictionary, means failure to act, perform, or participate, therefore in the case of Blenders Materials it means gray is what you get unless you do something about it.

The default dull gray color is what Blender uses so that it has something to show you.

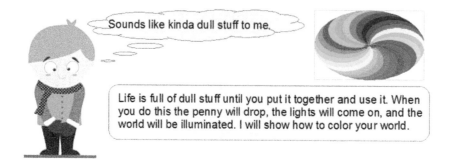

The Default Color

When you start Blender, the 3D Window has a Cube object in the center of the Scene. The Cube displays as the default gray color. The default Cube has this **Material** color **applied** to its surface. This is the only time that a Material color is actually **applied** to an object when it is entered into a scene. When you enter other objects, they automatically display with the same gray Material color but the color is not automatically applied. Blender just uses the gray color so that it has something to show you.

The best way to understand the application of materials is to work through an exercise.

The Materials Buttons

Materials (colors) are selected and applied using the Properties Window Materials buttons. The Properties Window is at the RHS of the screen. When the default Cube Object is selected, you see the Materials buttons as shown here. The buttons display because the Material is already applied to the default Cube Object.

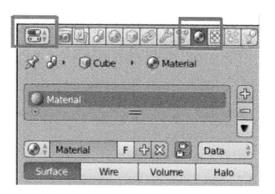

If you delete the Cube and add a new Object such as a UV Sphere, then the Materials buttons will display like this.

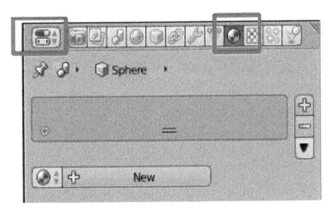

This display indicates that a Material **has not been applied**. The sphere shows as the default gray color because Blender uses this for something to show you in the 3D Window. The gray Material color is not applied. To apply a Material, you click on the New button. When you do this the button controls open in the Properties Window and, would you believe it, you get the dull gray default color.

Selecting a Material Color

The first thing you do when selecting a Material color is have your object/model selected in the 3D Window.

The Properties Window shows properties for the object selected in the 3D Window.

The Material color is going to be applied to the surface of the selected object. Remember the default Cube object already has the gray Material color applied so go get something else. A UV Sphere is good or you can use your airplane model, if you remember where the Blender file is saved.

Turn the page.

If you use a UV Sphere object, click on Smooth in the Tools Panel at the LHS of the 3D Window. This makes the surface of the sphere appear smooth and gives a better display when applying Materials.

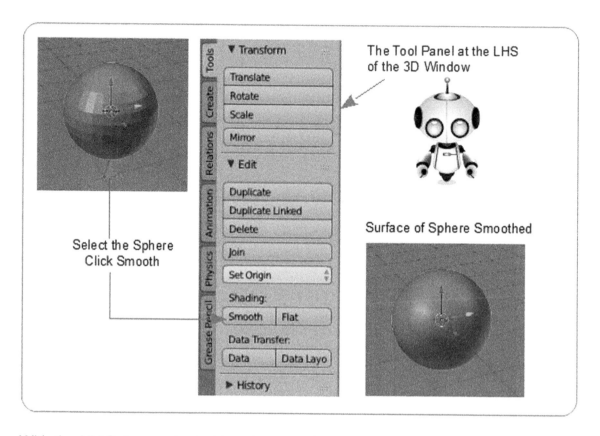

Select the Sphere
Click Smooth

The Tool Panel at the LHS
of the 3D Window

Surface of Sphere Smoothed

With the UV Sphere selected head over to the Properties Window and click on the Materials button. Click on the New button.

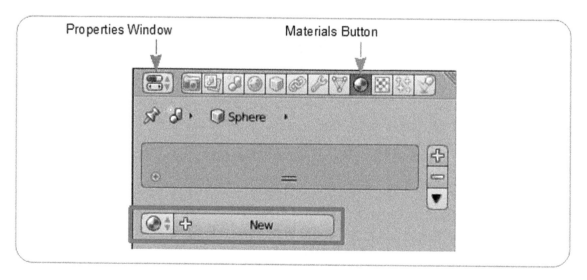

Properties Window

Materials Button

The Materials buttons for the UV Sphere will open showing the settings for the default gray color.

Material Buttons
(For the UV Sphere)

Click, hold, and drag the slider button up or down to adjust the brightness.

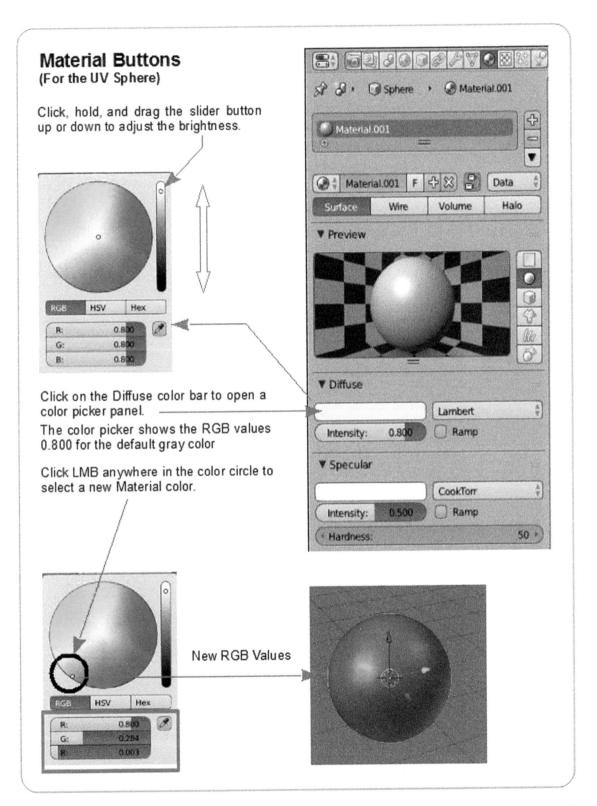

Click on the Diffuse color bar to open a color picker panel.

The color picker shows the RGB values 0.800 for the default gray color

Click LMB anywhere in the color circle to select a new Material color.

New RGB Values

What we have done so far is apply a Material (color) to the UV Sphere. By default, Blender applied the default gray Diffuse color. We changed this to a nice brown color.

You will notice that underneath the Diffuse tab is the Specular tab.

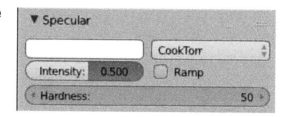

The Specular Material color is the color of reflected highlights on a surface. By default, this color is white. You see this as a white spot on the surface of the sphere. You can see it in the 3D Window and in the Preview tab. The Specular color can be changed the same way as the Diffuse Material color.

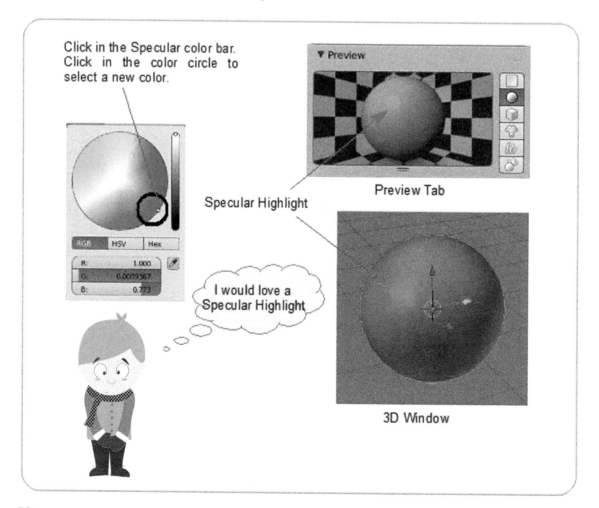

When you are adding Materials, you will probably invent some particular colors that you like and may want to use again. It is a good idea to record the RGB values, then you can enter the values and replicate the color at any time in the future.

More Materials

Besides Material colors, there is a lot more you can do to create stunning images. I will tell you about a few of the features to get you interested.

As a starting point, use the UV Sphere with its nice brown Diffuse color and whatever Specular color you have chosen.

In the 3D Window, deselect the UV Sphere (press the A Key). Add a new Plane object, scale it up and position it just below the UV Sphere as shown in the diagram.

At this point the Scene in the 3D Window has a UV Sphere object and a Plane object. There is also a Lamp providing light and a Camera. Another element in the composition is the background to the image.

The Lamp in the Scene is the default Spot Lamp in its default position with its default settings. Any of these defaults can be changed should you wish but for the exercise, leave them as they are. To produce a final image, we will alter Material values for the UV Sphere, the Plane, and the background. The Camera remains in its default position.

The UV Sphere: For the UV Sphere, use the settings previously set producing the nice brown Diffuse color for the surface and whatever Specular color you have chosen.

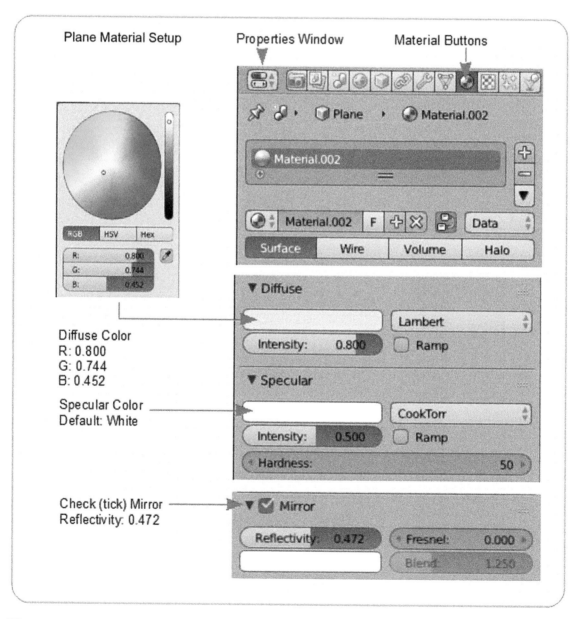

Plane Material Setup

Properties Window

Material Buttons

Diffuse Color
R: 0.800
G: 0.744
B: 0.452

Specular Color
Default: White

Check (tick) Mirror
Reflectivity: 0.472

The Plane: Select the Plane and set the Properties Window, Materials buttons as per the diagram on Page 78 opposite.

The Background: Background Materials are set in the Properties Window, World buttons.

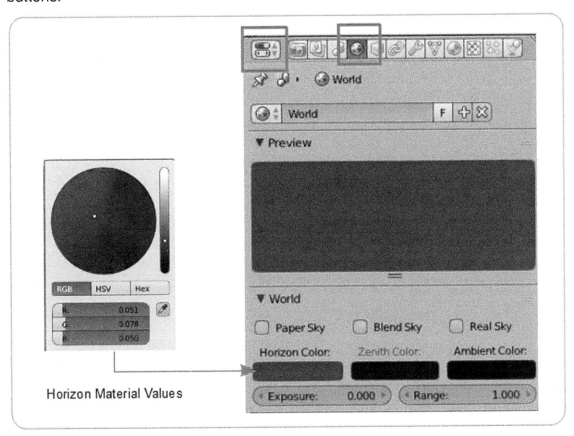

Horizon Material Values

The Final Image

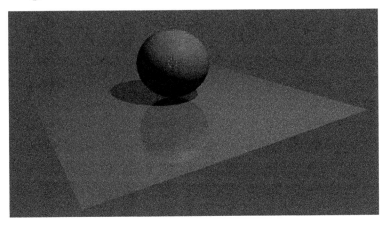

As you can see, there are many settings which you can play with to produce a variety of effects. Don't be afraid to experiment and try for yourself.

Lighting

In the real world the color of an object that you see is the result of light reflecting off its surface. What light is reflected depends on what part of the light spectrum is absorbed by the surface material and what the light consists of in the first place. Blender replicates this phenomenon on the computer screen, therefore lighting is an important part of composition. There are several Lamp types from which to choose, each of which has its own color and intensity settings. You can have multiple Lamps in a scene therefore the light combinations are limitless.

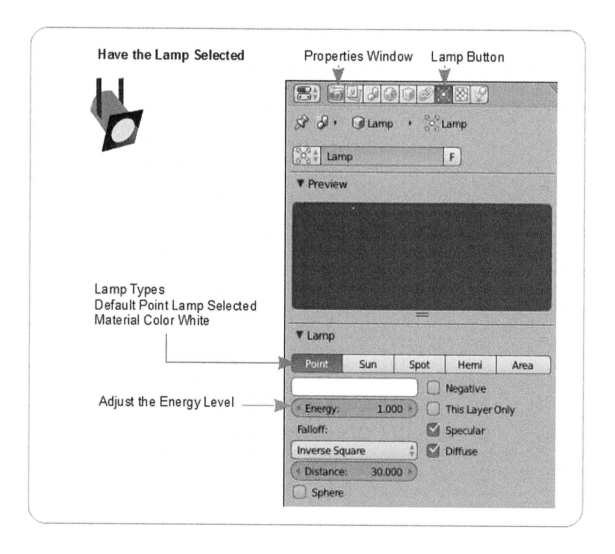

This has been the tip of the iceberg when considering Materials and you can see it is a fascinating and important part of the creation process. Up to this point I have been using the Blender Render system with Materials. The alternative is the Cycles Render system which has different controls and makes use of Blender's Node system. This opens a new can of worms which will have to wait for the time being.

Chapter 8
Textures

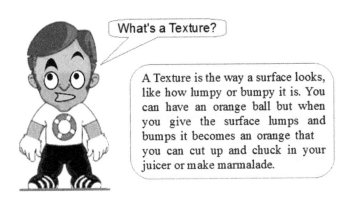

What's a Texture?

A Texture is the way a surface looks, like how lumpy or bumpy it is. You can have an orange ball but when you give the surface lumps and bumps it becomes an orange that you can cut up and chuck in your juicer or make marmalade.

The image shown above is a small JPEG image saved on the computer. To demonstrate the application of a **Texture** I will place this onto the surface of an Object. This is what is called applying an **Image Texture**. Blender has several in-built Textures called **Procedural Textures**, but we will use the Image Texture.

Start a new Blender Scene and add a UV Sphere object. You can delete the default Cube.

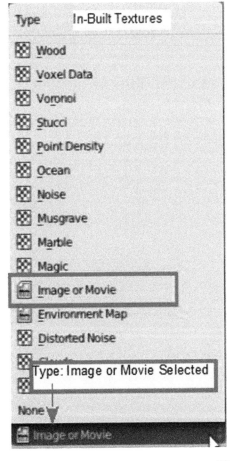

Type   In-Built Textures

- Wood
- Voxel Data
- Voronoi
- Stucci
- Point Density
- Ocean
- Noise
- Musgrave
- Marble
- Magic
- Image or Movie
- Environment Map
- Distorted Noise

Type: Image or Movie Selected

None

Image or Movie

With the UV Sphere selected in the 3D Window, click on **Smooth** in the Tool Panel, Tools tab at the LHS of the window.

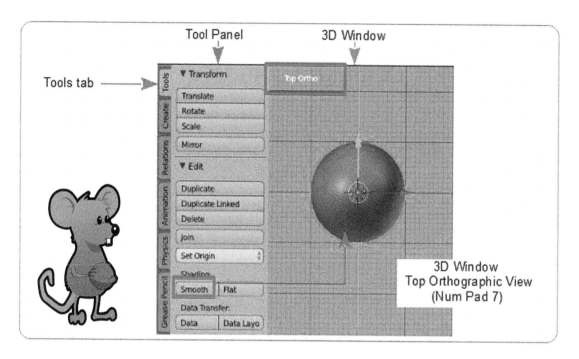

Press the **Tab** Key to place the UV Sphere in Edit Mode. Note: The Tool Panel changes. The UV Sphere is shown with its **Vertices** displayed. For this demonstration the default number of vertices is adequate. In the **Shading UVs tab**, click on **Unwrap**.

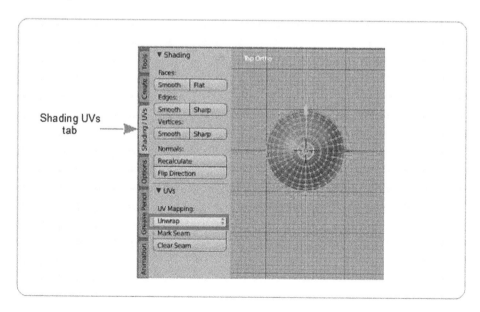

Clicking **Unwrap** opens a selection menu. Select **Sphere Projection**.

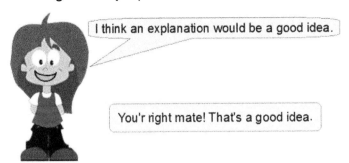

I think an explanation would be a good idea.

You'r right mate! That's a good idea.

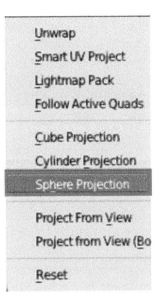

Unwrap

Smart UV Project

Lightmap Pack

Follow Active Quads

Cube Projection

Cylinder Projection

Sphere Projection

Project From View

Project from View (Bo

Reset

Smoothing you have seen before. This just makes the surface of the object (the UV Sphere) appear smooth which is good for seeing colors when they are applied.

Oh! By the way. Before I forget. Go ahead and apply a material to the UV Sphere. Just click the Materials button in the Properties Window and then click on New. Just as we did in the last chapter. The default gray will do fine.

Two Little Important Facts:

Before you can apply a Texture, you must apply a Material. It doesn't matter what the Material is because the Texture will override the Material.

Before you can apply a Texture, you must Unwrap the Object.

Unwrapping: is peeling off the surface of an object and laying it out flat so the Texture can be placed on the flat surface. We have unwrapped the UV Sphere's surface and you can see this if you open the UV Image Editor Window.

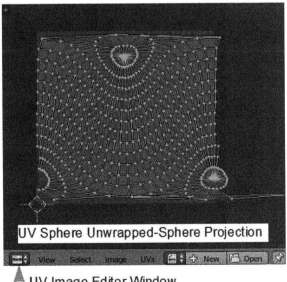

UV Sphere Unwrapped-Sphere Projection

UV Image Editor Window

Applying Texture

Make sure you have applied a Material. Textures are applied in the Properties Window—wait for it—Texture buttons.

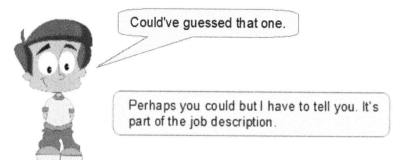

Could've guessed that one.

Perhaps you could but I have to tell you. It's part of the job description.

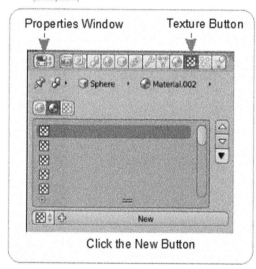

Properties Window   Texture Button

Click the New Button

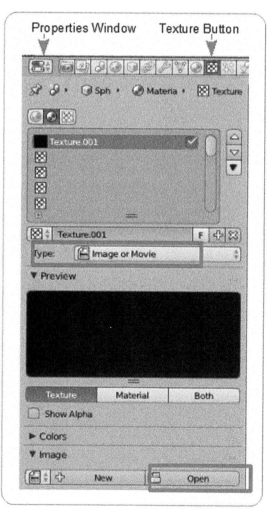

Properties Window   Texture Button

When you click the New button, the Texture buttons expand showing the controls for the Object that is selected in the 3D Window. By default the Texture Type, Image, or Movie is active. In the Preview tab, you see a black preview because you haven't selected a Texture Image at this point. To select an image to be used as a Texture, click on **Open** in the Image tab.

Clicking Open opens the File Browser Window. This is the same window you used when saving your work.

Selecting an Image as a Texture

In the File Browser Window, you navigate through your computer's file system to a folder containing the image you wish to use as a Texture. This could be a single image you have taken with a camera and saved, or a selection of Texture images you have downloaded. On my computer I have a folder named BLENDER_IMAGE_ TEXTURES which contains a whole selection of images. In the diagram, you can see the file names for each image. This is OK if you know what image you want to use, but if you are selecting an image at random it isn't very helpful.

Blender will help you. In the window header, click on the **Thumbnail** display option and you will see your image or images as **Thumbnails** (little pictures). Click on a picture and press (click) the Open Image button at the top RH of the screen.

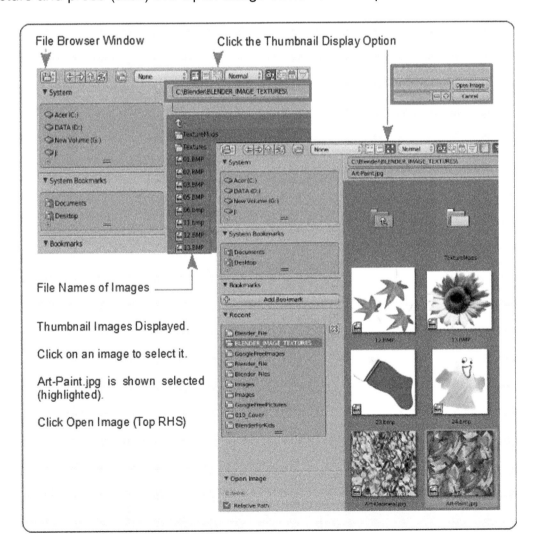

When you click Open Image, the screen reverts to the 3D Window and Properties Window.

In the Properties Window, Preview tab, you see the image you have selected as multiple copies spread across the panel.

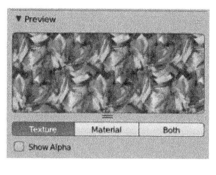

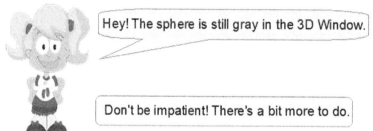

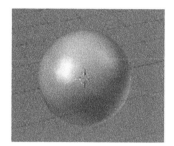

At this point, the 3D Window is in **Solid Viewport Shading** mode and probably in **User Perspective** view. Change to **Camera view** by pressing Num Pad 0.

You will see the gray UV Sphere in the window, inside a rectangle. Outside the rectangle the window is a dark shade of gray. The gray surround is called the **Passepartout**. This can be turned off but we won't worry about that right now.

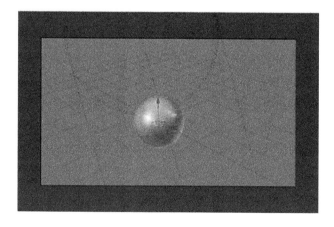

Even though you have applied a Texture to the 3D Window, it shows the sphere as the gray default color. This is to save computer power while you are constructing your scene. With only a UV Sphere, a Camera, and a Lamp in the scene it doesn't have much effect, but if you have a complicated scene with many objects and scenery, all with different Textures applied, then to show the Textures the computer would be in overdrive. Moving things in the scene will become very slow and jerky and, depending on your PC, it could freeze or crash.

Anyway! We want to see the Texture on the UV Sphere.

In the 3D Window header, click on the **Viewport Shading option** button and select **Rendered** from the menu.

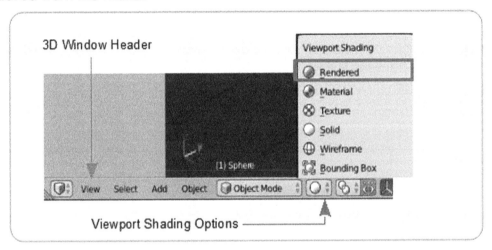

3D Window Header

Viewport Shading

Rendered
Material
Texture
Solid
Wireframe
Bounding Box

[1] Sphere

View   Select   Add   Object   Object Mode

Viewport Shading Options

In earlier versions of the BLENDER program, the Rendered Viewport Shading Option was not available. To see Texture, you had to Render an Image (Press F12). You can still do this but it is much more convenient to see changes to the scene Rendered as you work.

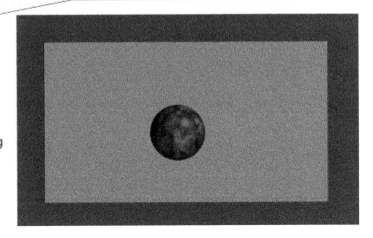

Rendered Viewport showing the Texture mapped to the surface of the UV Sphere.

Remember, this procedure can be used on any Object in the 3D Window. When I say Object I am referring to a Mesh Object. A Mesh Object is one where you see that it has Vertices when you Tab into Edit Mode. There are other types of Objects in Blender which are not Mesh Objects.

Surface Displacement

One more trick just to finish off.

A texture can be used to displace the vertices of a Mesh Object to give the surface lumps and bumps. In the Properties Window, Texture buttons, Influence tab, simply check (tick) Displace in the Geometry section and adjust the value.

Adjust the value by clicking in the **Displace** bar, holding and dragging the mouse left or right or clicking, pressing delete, and retyping a new value. Note: Values in sliders are not always infinitely variable. In the Displace Slider, the value is adjustable between +1.000 and –1.000.

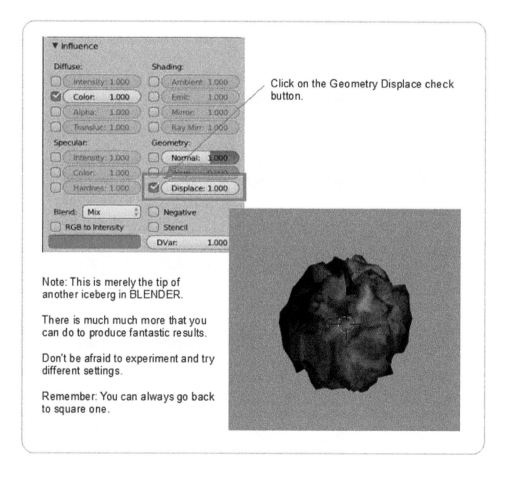

Click on the Geometry Displace check button.

Note: This is merely the tip of another iceberg in BLENDER.

There is much much more that you can do to produce fantastic results.

Don't be afraid to experiment and try different settings.

Remember: You can always go back to square one.

Texture Images as Scene Background

When I was showing you how to model something (the aircraft) an image was created with a colored background, and I showed you that an image could be used to create a background to the scene (clouds in the sky).

Go on the Internet and find yourself a nice picture of clouds in the sky like the one above.

I will use the picture as an **Image Texture**. In other words the picture will be used as a background for the image of the aircraft. Save the picture, and remember where you saved it.

Go back and find the Blender file you saved when you modeled your aircraft, and open the file.

Put the 3D Window into Camera view and have your aircraft model in the viewport. Make sure the model is **NOT** selected (press the A Key if it is).

Go to the **Properties Window, Texture buttons.** Click on the World Texture button (see diagram). Click on the **New** button to display the Texture tabs. The default Texture Type is Image or Movie.

If you click on Image or Movie, you will see a selection menu for a number of Texture options but you will be using the default setting.

World Texture Button

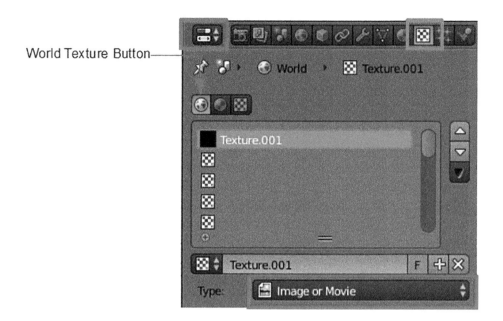

In the **Image tab**, click on **Open**. The File Browser Window opens. Find the cloud picture you saved, select it, and click open image. In the **Influence** tab, check (tick) **Horizon.**

When you render an image (press F12), you will see the clouds in the background of the image. With the 3D Window in Rendered Viewport Shading mode, you will see that the clouds are spread across the entire window and the Camera is only capturing a part of the Texture background.

If you want the Texture image to totally fit the background of the rendered image, you have to know the resolution of the texture image (the physical size in number of pixels wide and number of pixels high). You can then go to the Properties Window, Render buttons and change the values in the Dimensions tab, Resolution panel to match the resolution of the image.

Perhaps that's another story for later on.

Chapter 9
Downloading and Using
Models

Say hello to Zoe. Zoe is a cartoon character but she is also a **Model**. She is not one of your high-end fashion models who parade up and down a catwalk but she is a Blender model rigged for animation.

> Zoe was made by Pablo of Pablo Studios who has uploaded Zoe to the BLEND SWAP website. Zoe can be downloaded as 76271_Zoe.zip. Thank you, Pablo.

BLEND SWAP is one of numerous websites you can access and download models to use. Some websites ask you to pay for model downloads but BLEND SWAP doesn't. You do, however, have to register as a user and agree to their terms of use. Many models entail a lot of work so it is good to show appreciation.

How do I get Zoe?

Open your search engine and type:

www.blendswap.com/blends/view/76271

in the address bar.

The web address will take you directly to the download page for Zoe. Zoe is just one of many Blender files you can download from the site. To see other models, click on BLENDS in the header at the top of the page, then start scrolling through the pages.

To download Zoe click on the DOWNLOAD button. Remember you must be logged in to download which means you must be registered as a user.

When you download Zoe, you download a file name: 76271_Zoe.zip.

The .zip bit at the end tells you it is a compressed file which means it has been scrunched into a smaller file size to make it quicker to download. Guess What! You have to unscrunch the file to use it. To unscrunch (unzip) the file, you can use the program **WinZip** or **WinRar** or the free program **7-Zip**.

I will assume you can unscrunch the file or if not, get someone to do it for you. When it is unscrunched, you will have a Blender file named: Zoe.blend.

In Blender, open the file Zoe.blend to see Zoe in the 3D Window.

How to Use Zoe

If you take a close look at Zoe and rotate her in the 3D Window (click, hold, and drag MMB), you will see that she is surrounded by some strange looking shapes. Some are black and some are red. The white circle with the red arc located at her left (your right) ankle is the 3D Window Manipulation Widget. You can turn this off in the 3D Window header.

Zoom out in the window and you will also see that there is a **Camera** in the **Scene** pointing at Zoe and a Plane Object above her.

The Plane above is a **Light Source**.

What's a Light Source?

By default, a Blender scene contains a Point Lamp to provide illumination. Look at the Info Window header and you will see Cycles Render has been selected. Cycles is an alternative Rendering System to the default Blender Render. With Cycles, active Objects can be turned into light sources that produce fantastic lighting effects.

Take another look at the black and red shapes. These are control handles for posing the model. Posing means positioning the parts of the model to look the way you want it to look. With Zoe you move parts of her body to make her look cuter than she already is.

Remember that in Blender a model is a mesh object and Zoe is no exception.

The control handles are linked (associated with) parts of the mesh, such that when a handle is moved the associated mesh moves. Moving body parts and inserting keyframes at different positions in the Timeline Window is how you animate a figure to move. Posing and animating is a whole book load of information in itself, but to give you the idea perform the following.

Concentrate on Zoe's head. You will have to zoom in and rotate Zoe to see the close up images as shown in the diagrams. Change the 3D Window to Pose Mode then click, hold, and drag the control handles to see the body part move.

The control handle for Zoe's right eye.

Click and drag on the red and green arrows to move the right eye.

The control handle for Zoe's mouth.

Click and drag the green arrow down then up to open and close the mouth.

There are lots of handles to experiment and play with. Don't be afraid.

Have a go. See if you can place Zoe in an action pose like this one.

To use the Zoe Object, you can place other Objects in the Scene, add and arrange Lamps, add a Landscape, etc. and modify Zoe herself. If you Save the file you save all the additions and modifications, so in effect you lose the original file. Alternatively you can select the **Save As** option.

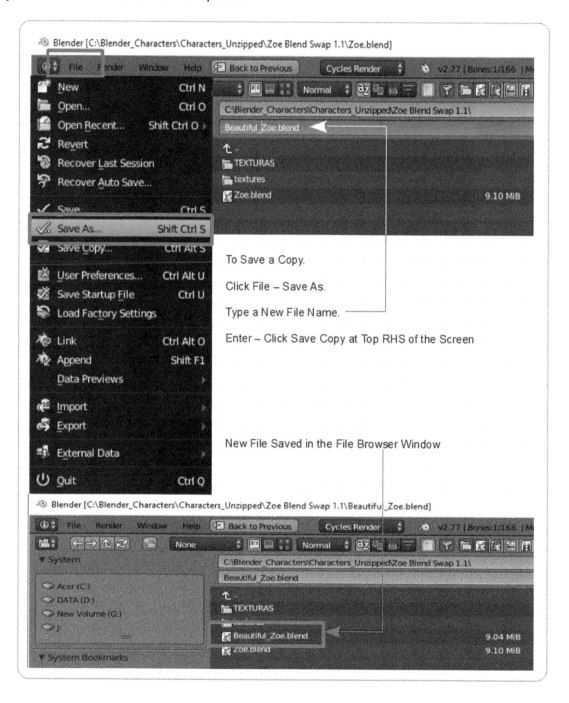

Using the Save As command saves a copy of the file and retains the original file for use at a later date.

Appending

A model in a Blender file can be Appended into a different file. This means you pluck the model from one file and place it into another file.

We can use your aircraft model as an example.

Make sure you understand how to navigate the file system (see Chapter 6).

Make sure you know where you have saved your aircraft file.

LET'S DO IT! Open a new Blender file and delete the Cube.

Have the **3D Window Cursor in the center of the Scene**. When you Append a model, it will be placed in the Scene at the location of the 3D Window Cursor.

> To accurately place the cursor, press Shift + S Key to get the Snap menu and select Cursor to Center.

> Appending is very much like copying and pasting from one file to another and, you guessed it, there are more ways than one to do this. It makes life interesting.

Your aircraft model is very simple. This is a good place to start for Appending.

When you made the model it was constructed from a Sphere Object and I purposely didn't provide any instruction on renaming it to anything else. Consequently, your aircraft model is named **Sphere** in your aircraft Blender file. This is OK as long as you remember the name.

Have a new blender file opened and deleted the default Cube. Your 3D Window Cursor is located at the center of the Scene.

It is, isn't it?

In the 3D Window header, click on File and select Append from the menu that displays.

Clicking Append opens the File Browser Window where you navigate to your aircraft Blender file.

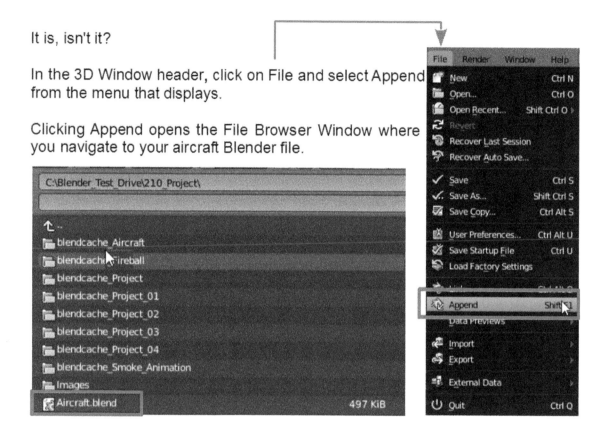

As you can see above, my Aircraft.blend file is saved in:

C:\Blender_Test_Drive\210_Project\

Click on the aircraft file to show the folders contained within the file.

Click on the Object folder and select Sphere.

Click on Append from Library in the upper right hand corner of the window.

Bingo! Your aircraft model is in the Scene.

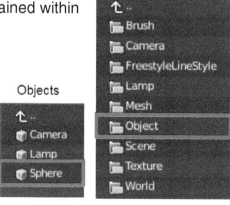

Appending a simple model or object into a file is fairly straightforward. Complex models like Zoe are not quite so easy to append.

At the beginning of Chapter I said Zoe was a model rigged for animation. By that I meant, the model came intact with control handles for posing, linked to the mesh. When a control handle is moved, the mesh moves.

The more traditional method of rigging a character model for posing and animating is to employ, what is termed, an Armature. An Armature is like a bone skeleton. In fact the parts of an Armature are called Bones.

To show you what I mean I have downloaded another model named "Mr. **Comic**."

The web address for the model download is:

www.blendswap.com/blends/view/23500

Say hello to Mr. Comic.

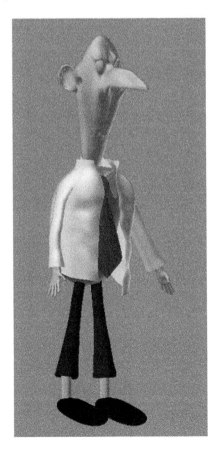

Comic has been uploaded to the Blend Swap website by Stalk.

When you have downloaded the zip file and unzipped, you have the Blender file named comic.blend. When the file is opened the 3D Window is in Camera Perspective view and you see Mr. Comic with some weird black stick lines connected by dots showing inside his body. This is the Armature.

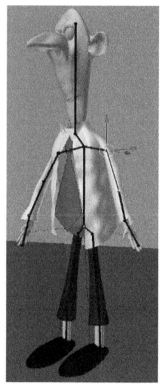 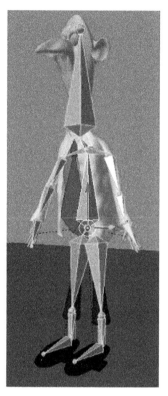 

Stick   Octahedral   B-Bone

Armatures can be displayed in different ways but for the demonstration I will use the stick configuration.

The Armature sticks, or to be precise the bones, are linked to parts of the mesh just like the control handles in the Zoe model. You select a bone and move it to make the mesh move.

The figure on the left shows an arm bone selected (click RMB to select).

When the Blender file is first opened, the 3D Window is in Object Mode. When you select a bone, this changes to Pose Mode.

Mr. Comic is still a relatively simple model but it is more complicated than your aircraft model. When you appended the aircraft, you found the Sphere Object in the File Browser Window. If you go looking for Mr. Comic, you will not find his name listed or anything else that is meaningful.

To get Mr. Comic into another Blender file, you use a cut-and-paste method.

With the comic.blend file opened and the 3D Window in Camera Perspective View, you select the model by pressing the B Key (Box select) and dragging a rectangle around Mr. Comic. **BUT!** Before you do, RMB click on the floor plane and delete it from the Scene.

Edge of Camera View

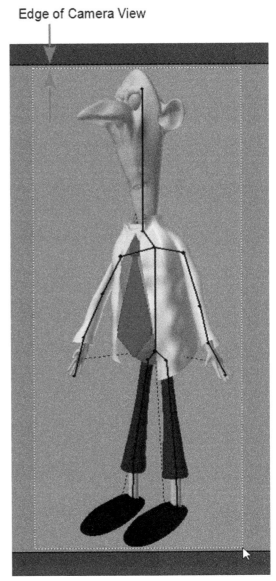

Make sure you are inside the Camera View otherwise you will also select the Camera.

With Mr. Comic selected, press Ctrl + C (copy). In the Info Window header, you will see "Copied selected to buffer" display. Wait until this disappears.

In the Info Window header, click in File— New—Reload Start Up File.

In the new Blender Window that opens, delete the default Cube object, then press Ctrl + V (paste).

There you have it Mr. Comic in a new Scene ready to go.

Chapter 10
Spin Magic

Blender has two quick tools for creating circular Objects called **Spin** and **Screw**. Spin extrudes and duplicates vertices around a center point, while Screw does the same thing and offsets the duplication at the same time. The center point in, both cases, is the **3D Window Cursor**. To make sense of these processes, follow the procedures precisely. Both the position of the 3D Window Cursor and how the Viewport is arranged are important.

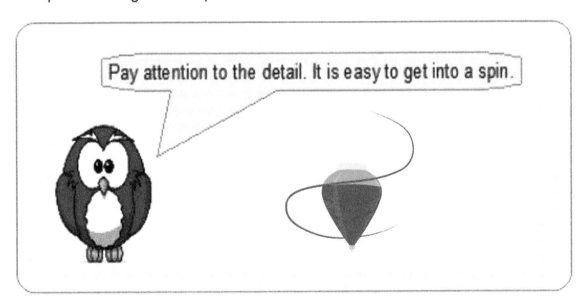

Pay attention to the detail. It is easy to get into a spin.

The Spin Tool

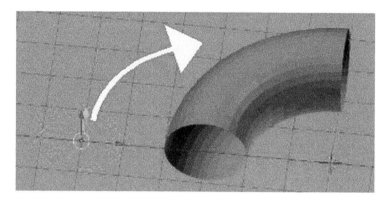

To show how **Spin** works, start by simply making a doughnut from a circle. The **Circle Object** will be the cross section profile for the doughnut. The cross section profile for spinning can be any shape you like, formed by a string of vertices. A circular shape is a closed loop of vertices but this doesn't have to be the case. Any string will work. In fact you can spin any shape, even an Object.

Use a **Circle Object** so you see what is shown in the diagrams. You can experiment later.

Start a new Blender **Scene**, delete the default **Cub**e and add a **Circle Object**.

When you add a Circle Object it always presents, lying flat, in **Top Orthographic View**. Make it stand on edge so you see it in **Front Orthographic View**. With the circle selected, press the R Key + X Key + 90, which tells Blender to Rotate about the X axis, 90°.

With the circle selected, in **Object Mode**, move it four grid units to the left and then **Tab into Edit Mode**.

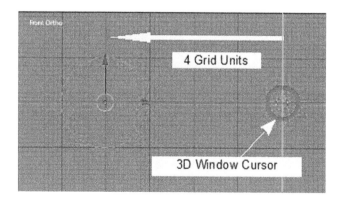

The distance moved doesn't have to be exact but make sure the **3D Window Cursor** remains at the center of the **Scene**. If you have clicked somewhere in the 3D Window, it will be wherever you clicked. To get it back to the center, press Shift + S key and select **Cursor to Center** from the menu that displays.

Change the 3D Window to **Top Orthographic View**.

To spin the profile, simply press **Spin** in the **Tool Panel, Tools tab** at the LHS of the 3D Window.

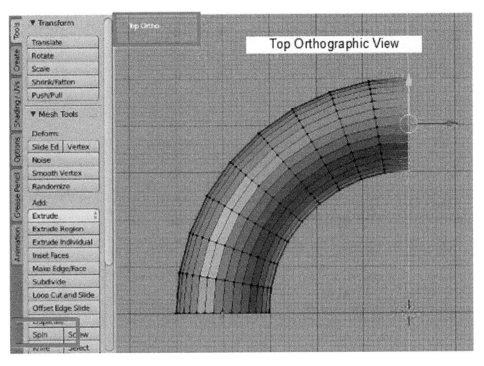

Top Orthographic View

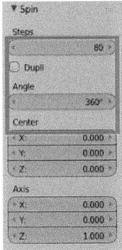

When **Spin** is pressed, the profile is extruded around a circular arc of 90°.

The Spin tool panel displays in the **Tool Panel** at the lower LHS of the Screen.

By default, the rotation is 90° and there are nine steps in the extrusion. Change the steps to 80 and the angle to 360° to form a complete circle. More Steps creates a smoother Object.

With any extrusion, you finish up with the original set of vertices plus the extruded vertices, so in the closed circle with 80 Steps you have 81 sets of vertices, with the last set superimposed over the original. You have doubled up.

In the **Tool Panel**, click on **Remove Doubles**.

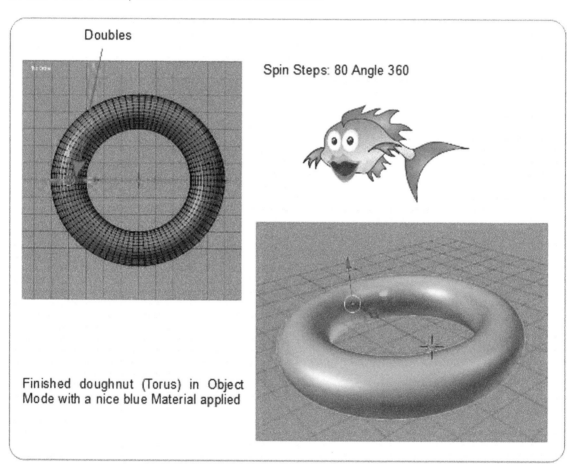

Doubles

Spin Steps: 80 Angle 360

Finished doughnut (Torus) in Object Mode with a nice blue Material applied

More Spin

A doughnut is a good starting point for the Spin Tool, but you could just as well have added a **Torus Object** to your Scene. Let's make something a little more exciting. Make a simple bowl.

The first thing to do is make a cross section profile of the bowl.

Start a new Blender Scene, delete the Cube Object and add a Plane Object. The Plane will be presented laid flat on the mid-plane of the Scene. Flip it up on edge, press R Key + X Key + 90.

Change the 3D Window to **Front Orthographic View** and tab into **Edit Mode**.

In Edit Mode, move the vertices **one Blender Grid Unit** to the left. To accurately position the vertices, press the **N Key** to open the **Object Properties Panel** on the RHS of the window (press the N Key again to close the panel). In the panel, in the **Transform tab,** make the **X Median** value: –1.00000, that is, **minus one**.

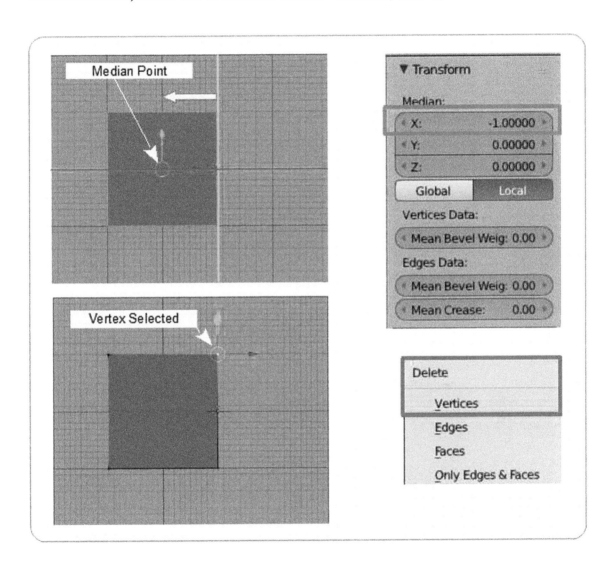

The **Median** is the middle of the selected group of vertices. The **Manipulation Widget** locates at the **Median Point when in Edit Mode**. With a square Plane Object, the Median Point is slap bang in the center.

Press the A Key to deselect the Vertices, then RMB click on a single Vertex. Press the X Key and select Delete Vertices in the menu that displays. You now have an open string consisting of three vertices. This is the starting point for creating your bowl cross section profile.

Make particular note that the lower RH vertex is located on the center of the vertical Z axis of the Scene. This coincides with the center of the 3D Window cursor.

Arrange and add vertices, as shown in the diagrams, to form a profile.

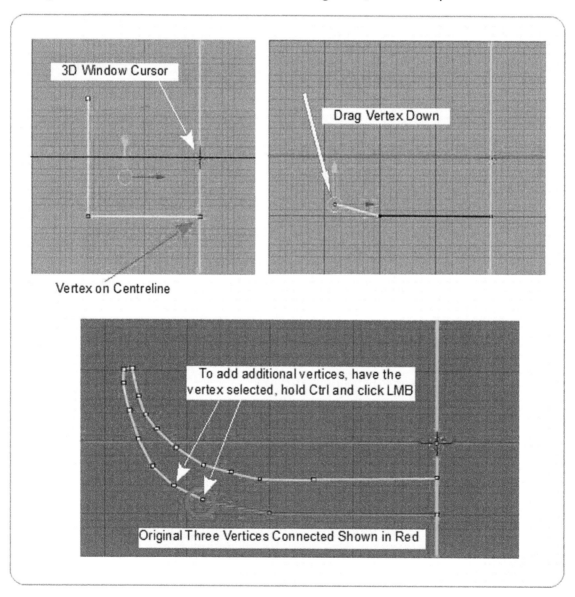

With the profile completed and all vertices selected, in **Edit Mode**, press **Num Pad 7** to place the 3D Window in **Top Orthographic View**. In the **Tool Panel, Tools tab**, click on **Spin**. Make sure the 3D Window Cursor is at the center of the Scene.

In the Spin Tool Panel, increase the steps and make the angle 360°. Remove Doubles.

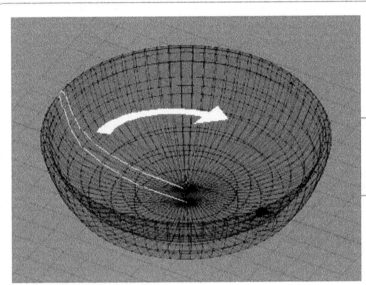

Press Spin to spin the profile.

The view is shown in Wireframe mode.

Tab to Object Mode, click on Smooth in the Tools Panel, add a Material and rotate the view to see your bow.

The Screw Tool

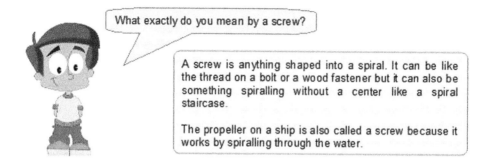

What exactly do you mean by a screw?

A screw is anything shaped into a spiral. It can be like the thread on a bolt or a wood fastener but it can also be something spiralling without a center like a spiral staircase.

The propeller on a ship is also called a screw because it works by spiralling through the water.

Creating a screw or spiral in Blender is similar to spinning in that the spiral takes place about the center of the 3D Window Cursor. The spiral is also affected by whatever 3D Window Viewport you have at the time. To see how to spiral, be in the **Front Orthographic View**.

Start a new Blender Scene and delete the default Cube Object. Put the viewport in **Front Orthographic View** (press Num Pad 1).

Add a Circle Object. The circle will be presented at the location of the 3D Window Cursor, which, hopefully, is at the center of the Scene. If it isn't, press Shift + S Key and select Cursor to Center from the menu. If you do this after you have added the circle, press Shift + S Key and select Object to Cursor. This is an accurate way of locating anything at the center of the Scene.

The Circle Object is always presented flat in Top Orthographic View, so flip it on edge (R + X + 90) so you see it in the Front Orthographic View.

With the Circle Object selected (Object Mode), move the circle five grid units to the left.

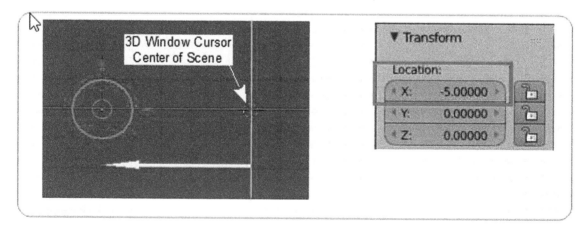

Moving the circle doesn't have to be accurate, but if it had to be, you can use the **Object Properties Panel**. This panel is hidden from view by default. To display it press the **N Key**. Pressing the **N Key** a second time will hide the panel (saves room in the 3D Window).

With the Object Properties Panel open in the **Transform tab,** change the **Location X** value to –5.00000 (minus 5).

With the circle relocated, Tab into Edit Mode, and with the circle still selected (vertices showing orange) add a Plane Object to the Scene. The Plane is entered at the location of the 3D Window Cursor at the center of the Scene. It is also entered lying flat when in Top Orthographic View so flip it on its edge so we can see it in Front view (R + X + 90). Both the Circle and the Plane are selected. Press the A Key to deselect then press the B Key and drag a rectangle around the Plane to select the Plane. Move the Plane one grid unit to the right.

You want the left-hand edge of the Plane to be exactly on the vertical Z axis of the 3D Window. Go to the Object Properties Panel again (N Key to display) and in the Transform tab change the Median X value to 1.000.

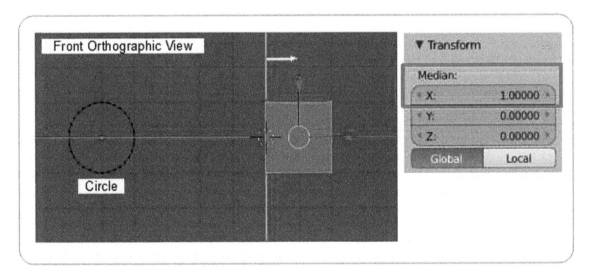

What you are about to do is make a single vertical line consisting of two vertices. The length of this line determines the **Pitch of the Screw** (vertical length/height of the spiral).

Press the A Key to deselect the Plane then the B Key and drag a rectangle around the RH edge. With the RH edge selected, press the X Key to delete. You are left with the single line on the vertical Z axis.

While it is still selected press the S Key, drag the Mouse and scale the line up so that it is approximately four grid units long.

Press the A Key to deselect then press A Key again to select the Circle and the Line.

With both the Circle and the Line selected, click on the Screw button in the Tool Panel, Tools tab at the LHS of the 3D Window.

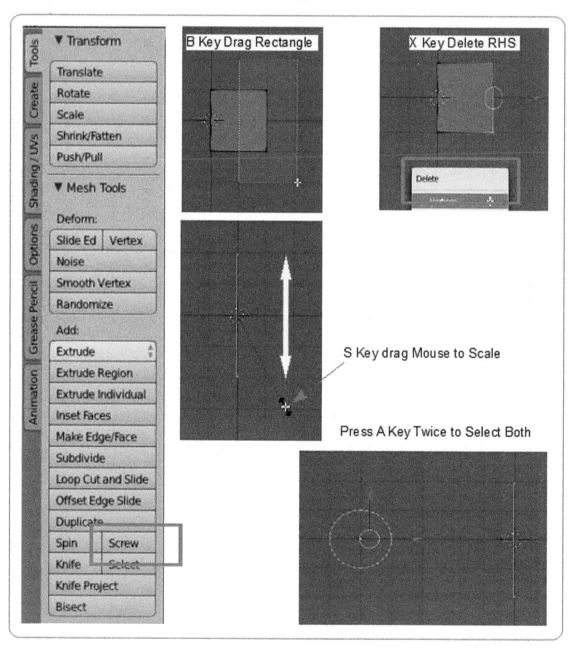

The screw is generated, and the **Screw Panel** displays at the lower LHS of the 3D Window.

Adjust the **Steps** value to add more vertices and smooth the screw and increase the **Turns** value to increase the number of turns (spirals).

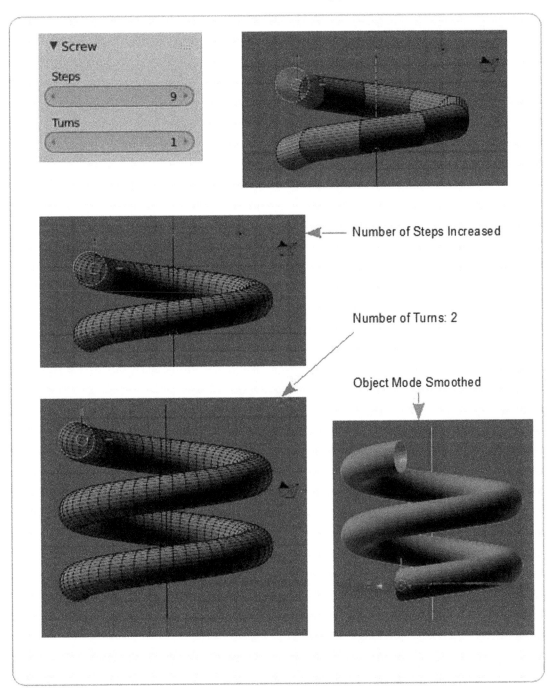

▼ Screw

Steps

9

Turns

1

Number of Steps Increased

Number of Turns: 2

Object Mode Smoothed

Chapter 11
Quick Fluid

I know you like the quick stuff, so I will show you how to make a **Fluid Simulation**. The fluid can be water, milk, oil, honey, in fact anything that flows.

This will be a very quick demonstration of the **Quick Fluid** method. It is only intended to show you one of Blender's features and encourage you to pursue further studies.

Open a new Blender Scene with the default **Cube Object**. With the Cube selected, press the **Space Bar** and type **Quick Fluid in** the search window that displays. Select **Quick Fluid** from the options. What you see in the **3D Window** immediately changes.

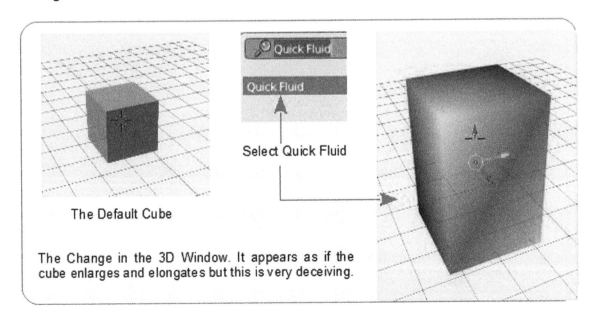

The Default Cube

Select Quick Fluid

The Change in the 3D Window. It appears as if the cube enlarges and elongates but this is very deceiving.

What actually happens is, the **Cube Object** has become a **Fluid Object** and has been surrounded by a cuboid. The cuboid is called a **Domain** and it represents a cubic volume of space in which the fluid simulation will take place. Change the **3D Window** from **Solid Display** mode to **Wireframe Display** mode.

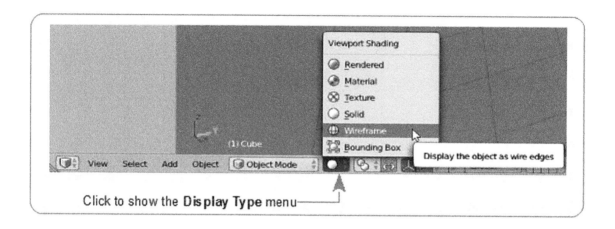

Click to show the **Display Type** menu

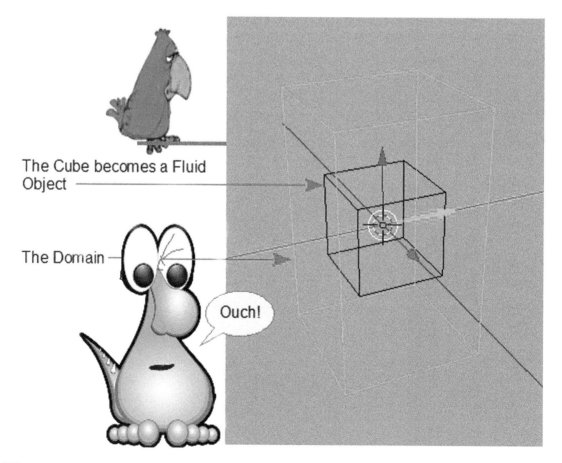

The Cube becomes a Fluid Object

The Domain

Ouch!

Look in the bottom LHS of the **3D Window** to see the **Quick Fluid tab**. Place a tick (click) in **Start Fluid bake** and wait. This is like baking a cake. You just have to be patient and wait until the cake is cooked. Look at the top of the **3D Window** and you will see a progress bar with a percentage value showing. When the cake is baked, the progress bar disappears.

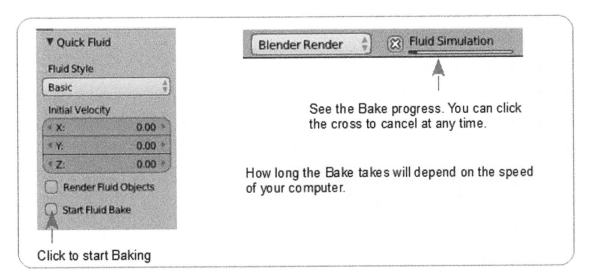

Change back to Solid Viewport Shading. In the Timeline Window, click Play to see the fluid descend inside the domain, splash, and come to rest.

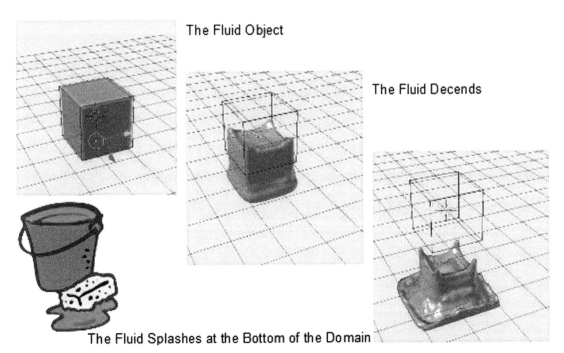

The Fluid Object

The Fluid Decends

The Fluid Splashes at the Bottom of the Domain

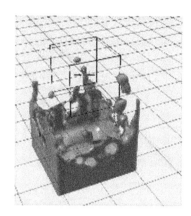

Fluid Splashes Up inside the Domain

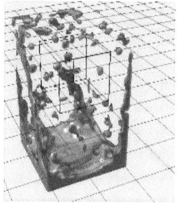

Way Way Up

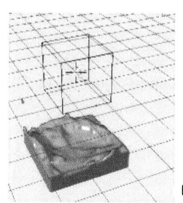

Splashes Fall Down Again

Fluid Comes to Rest

Many interesting effects can be created with **Fluid Simulation**.

Objects and the Domain can be altered which affects how the Fluid flows. The Fluid Object could be hidden inside a model of a tap or pipe, simulating the fluid exiting. There are viscosity settings for fluid which determine what type of fluid is being simulated. The color of the fluid can be varied. Other objects can be placed inside the domain to act as obstacles which the fluid has to flow around or to act as containers to catch the fluid.

There are many settings for fantastic effects for you to discover.

Chapter 12
Animation

This is one of the best parts of Blender. This is where you get to make things move about.

You have already seen things move when you use quick methods to make fire and smoke and explode, but I know you want to make your own models fly.

Let's begin with your super duper aircraft that you saved.

You did save it, didn't you!?

Never mind I will start off with something else anyway.

This is another case of learning to walk before you can fly.

Making things move about in computer graphics is called **Animation**.

Animation began when someone drew a whole bunch of pictures of something, with each picture being just a little bit different. They then flipped through the pictures very quickly and saw the illusion of their moving.

Picture cards turned into little bits called **Frames** on a long strip of celluloid (a movie reel) which had light shining through that projected the image onto a screen.

Today the images are stored as digital data in a computer and displayed on your monitor.

> Digital Data is thousands of 0 and 1 combinations like: 0100, 1010, 1101, 0010, etc, which tells the computer to put tiny colored squares on your screen that make up a picture.

The little squares are called **Pixels**.

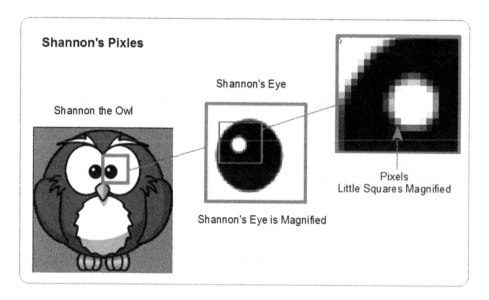

Your First Animation

Animation is the art of making you think you see something move. I will show you how this is done in Blender by making the default Cube Object in the default scene move.

Open a new Blender scene. Move the Cube, using the Widget, to the back of the Grid.

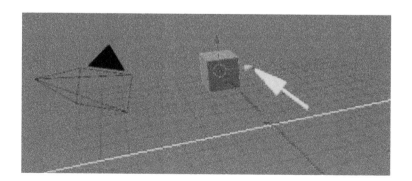

Look in the Timeline Window and note that the cursor (green line) is at Frame 1.

Place your Mouse Cursor in the 3D Window and press the I Key. In the menu that displays select (click) Location.

Move the Cube to the front of the Grid.

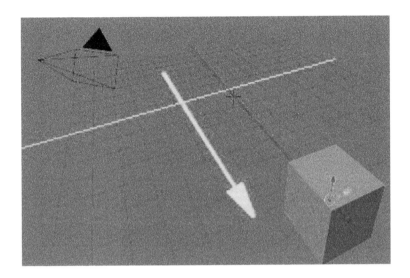

In the Timeline Window, move the cursor (green line) to Frame 60. You can move the cursor to any frame you like but 60 will give you a good demo.

With the Cube at the front of the Grid and the Timeline Cursor at Frame 60, put the Mouse cursor in the 3D Window and press the I Key again. Select Location from the menu.

In the Timeline Window, press the Go To Start button. Press the Play button to see the Cube move from the back of the Grid to the front.

No! THAT IS NOT IT!

Is that it?

This is the very very beginning. The animation has shown a simple translation (movement) of an Object.

I know you are itching to do something fantastical BUT!

Have you found where you saved your model of the aircraft?

While you are looking for it I will explain a little bit about the animation.

What you did was locate the **Cube** at the back of the **Grid** in the **3D Window**. In the Timeline Window, you placed the cursor at Frame 1. You then pressed the I Key and clicked in Location. Pressing the I Key and selecting Location inserted a **Keyframe** at Frame 1. You then relocated the Cube to the front of the Grid and placed another **Keyframe** at Frame 60.

Placing **Keyframes** tells Blender how to display the Cube at Frame 1 and Frame 60. Blender automatically works out how to display the Cube at all the in-between frames.

When you play the animation, all the Frames flash on the screen so you think the Cube is moving.

Oh! You have found your aircraft file at last. I can move on.

You could use the Cube and make it fly around but using the flying machine adds realism to the animation. Some simple things can look fantastic. Animating something to move in a straight line is relatively simple. As well as animating the location of an object, you may also animate the scale (size) and rotation and many other things. When you press the I Key to insert Keyframes, you see the different options in the selection menu:

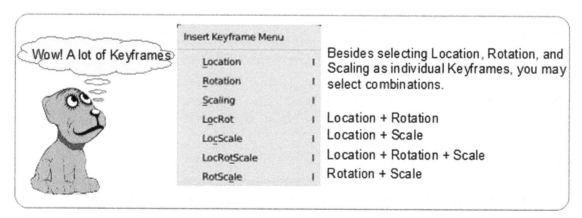

Yes, to make an object move, spin around, and change size during an animation, you would have to insert lots and lots of Keyframes.

This is another DON'T PANIC situation, just strap yourself in and fly with the instructions. At first this will probably appear to be a long and tedious process because you have to find the buttons to press and where to enter values. At the same time you have to understand what is going on. It will become simpler when you have practiced a bit and are familiar with the interface.

Let's get going.

Start-up Blender and open your aircraft file with your model in it. In Top Orthographic view (Num Pad 7), you should have a view as shown in the diagram.

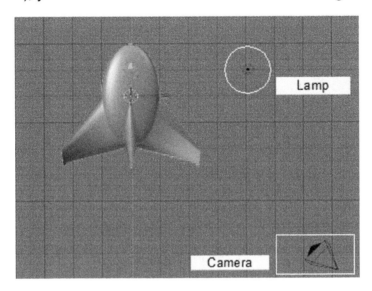

Make a note that the Camera is pointing toward your aircraft and in Camera View (Num Pad 0) you should see something like this.

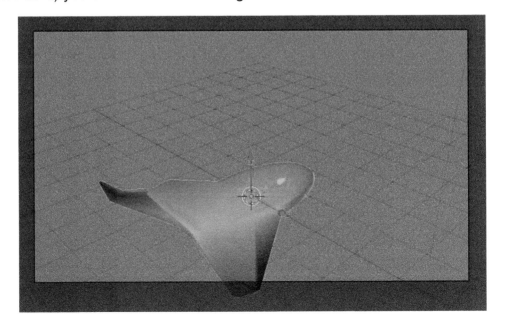

Place the 3D Window in Top Orthographic view (Num Pad 7).

With the Mouse Cursor in the 3D Window, press Shift + A Key and in the menu that displays, click **Curve** then **Circle**. This adds a **Bezier Circle** to the scene. In Blender, all the Curve options are **Paths**, which can be used for animating objects. They also have other uses, but I will not go into that at this time.

You are about to make your aircraft follow a Path. This means you will create an imaginary track in space which the aircraft flies along. You will use the Bezier Circle as the Path.

When you enter the Bezier Circle into the scene, it is one Blender unit in diameter. When you modeled the aircraft, you didn't consider what size it was since it was the only object in the scene. You began with a UV Sphere which by default was one Blender unit in diameter. You elongated the sphere on the Y axis and scaled it down on the Z axis. It remains at one Blender unit wide on the X axis. Therefore in width it is the same as the Bezier Circle.

You can see the relationship in Top Orthographic view with the 3D Window in Wireframe Viewport Shading Mode. Viewport Shading is the way in which the 3D Window displays the scene.

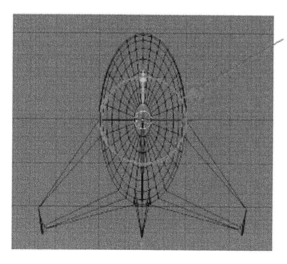

Bezier Circle One Unit
in Diameter

When it is important to know the size of one object relative to another or how far away something is, Blender has an Object Properties panel which shows you the relative dimensions. With the Mouse Cursor in the 3D Window, press the N Key and the panel will open on the RHS of the window. The important thing to remember is that all the values shown in the panel apply to the object that you have selected at the time. With the Bezier Circle selected, you will see the Scale: X, Y, and Z values 1.000. If you select the model of the aircraft (click RMB), you will see Scale: X 1.000, Y 2.000, and Z 0.357. The Z axis value will depend on how much you squished the UV Sphere.

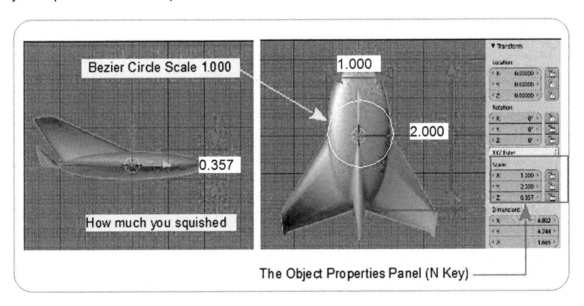

The Object Properties Panel (N Key)

To use the **Bezier Circle** as a Path for the aircraft to follow, you want it to be way bigger than 1.000. Maybe 40 times as big. Select the Bezier Circle. The Object Properties Panel will show the Scale values for the circle. They will be 1.000 for X, Y, and Z. The Z value doesn't mean anything since a circle in our case is just a circle. It is 1.000 wide (X) by 1.000 high (Y) but it has no thickness (Z).

To make the circle bigger, press the S Key and drag the mouse or press the S Key then 40. If you drag the mouse, watch the X, Y, and Z values increase as you drag. When they approach 40, click to release the mouse button. In either case, the circle is going to be displayed off the screen. Zoom out in the 3D Window until you see the **Bezier Circle**. Your aircraft will be very tiny.

A **Bezier** curve is a parametric curve frequently used in computer graphics and related fields. Generalizations of **Bezier** curves to higher dimensions are called **Bezier** surfaces, of which the **Bezier** triangle is a special case. The circle we are using is also a curve, therefore we have **Bezier Circle**.

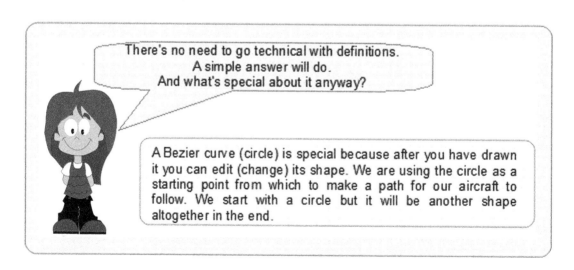

The Bezier Circle

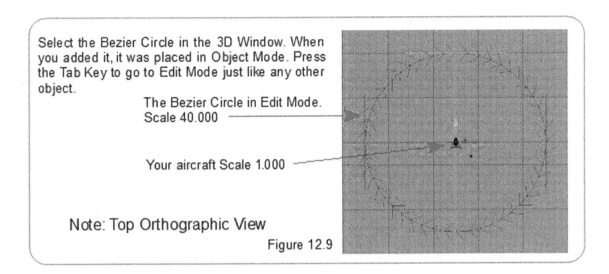

In Edit mode, the circle displays with chevrons spaced around the circle. Remember the circle is a Path. The chevrons point in the direction in which an object will travel when it is animated to follow the path. At four points around the circumference of the circle, you will see yellow (orange) lines with a point in the center of the line and points at each end. These lines are manipulation Handles (similar to the Manipulation Widget). You click LMB on a Handle to select it. When it is selected, the Manipulation Widget locates at the center point of the handle.

A circle is OK for a Path but a different shape is more interesting.

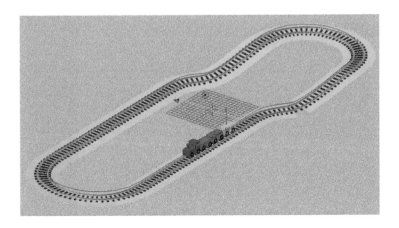

Change the Curve Shape

Select the curve (Circle) in Object Mode and tab into Edit Mode.

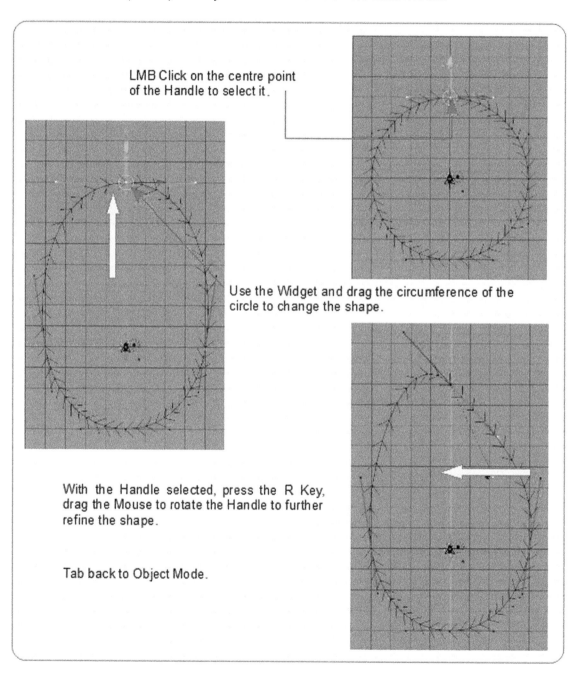

LMB Click on the centre point
of the Handle to select it.

Use the Widget and drag the circumference of the
circle to change the shape.

With the Handle selected, press the R Key,
drag the Mouse to rotate the Handle to further
refine the shape.

Tab back to Object Mode.

The Path in Object Mode

To make the aircraft follow the Path, you have to apply a Constraint. The aircraft is constrained to the Path.

The Constraint is applied in the Properties Window, Constraint buttons panel.

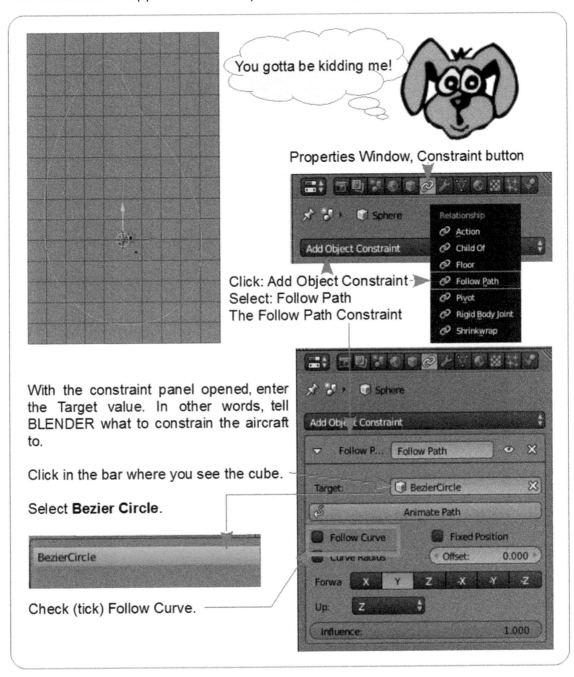

You gotta be kidding me!

Properties Window, Constraint button

Click: Add Object Constraint
Select: Follow Path
The Follow Path Constraint

With the constraint panel opened, enter the Target value. In other words, tell BLENDER what to constrain the aircraft to.

Click in the bar where you see the cube.

Select **Bezier Circle**.

BezierCircle

Check (tick) Follow Curve.

When you set the constraint, your aircraft will relocate from the center of the scene to the start point on the Curve Path. Note, however, it is pointing along the Y axis at right angles to the direction of the Path. To correct this, check (place a tick by clicking) **Follow Curve** in the **Constraint Panel**.

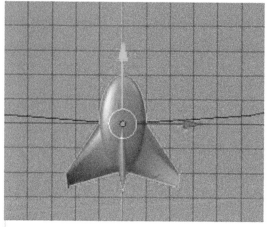

Pointing Along the Y Axis   Pointing in the Direction of the Path

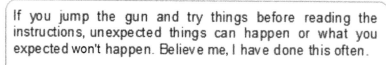

I pressed the Play button in the Timeline Window and nothing happened.

If you jump the gun and try things before reading the instructions, unexpected things can happen or what you expected won't happen. Believe me, I have done this often.

In your excitement, you forgot all about **Keyframes**.

You are producing an animation and you have to set the **Keyframes**. This is a **Path Animation** so you have to tell Blender where the aircraft is at the start and end of the Path.

You previously pressed the **I Key** to enter **Keyframes** with the selected object at different locations and at different frames in the animation. In **Path Animation**, you do this in a different way.

There are many things in Blender which may be animated and this is an example of the method used.

Deselect the aircraft (A Key) and select (click RMB) the **Curve Path** (Bezier Circle).

With the curve selected, **Tab** (press Tab) into Edit Mode to see the aircraft pointing in the direction of movement along the Path.

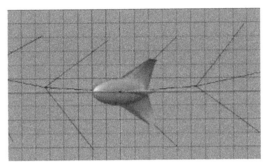

Aircraft on the Path—Path in Edit Mode

Tab back to Object mode. Remember the Path is selected.

Go to the Properties Window, Object data buttons. Pressing this button opens panels and tabs with information about the selected object in the 3D Window. Look down the panel and find the **Path Animation tab**.

Disregard the Frames: value for the time being.

Note the **Evaluation Time** value: 0.000. This is telling you that you are at the start of the Path at the start of the animation. The value is a percentage. At the start, this is 0%.

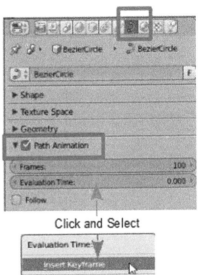

Click and Select

To enter a Keyframe at the start position (0.000%), click RMB on the Evaluation Time bar and select Insert Keyframe in the menu that displays.

The Evaluation Time bar will turn yellow indicating that a Keyframe has been set.

In the Timeline Window, press the **Go To Last Frame** button.

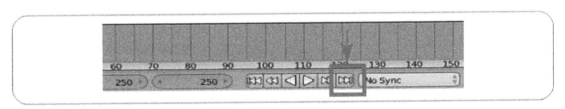

In the Path Animation tab, change the Evaluation Time to: 100.000 (100%). Click RMB and enter a second Keyframe.

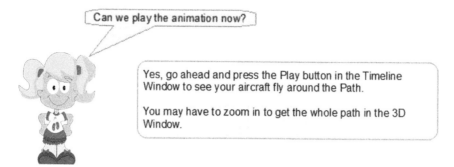

Can we play the animation now?

Yes, go ahead and press the Play button in the Timeline Window to see your aircraft fly around the Path.

You may have to zoom in to get the whole path in the 3D Window.

Remember when you placed the Bezier Circle in Edit mode and moved the Control Handle. You can go back and reshape the Curve Path at any time and this means you can reshape it on the X, Y, and Z axes. Reshaping on the Z axis means your aircraft flies up or down in the scene.

Camera View: You previously saw a picture of the aircraft in Camera View (Num Pad 0). If you switch to Camera View, now you won't see anything because the Camera is pointing at the spot where the aircraft was located in the beginning. It has been relocated to the start of the Path.

Seeing the aircraft fly around the Path in the 3D Window is OK for setting up the action but at some stage you will want to make a movie of the animation, and for that you will want your actor to be in the shot. In this case, the aircraft is the actor.

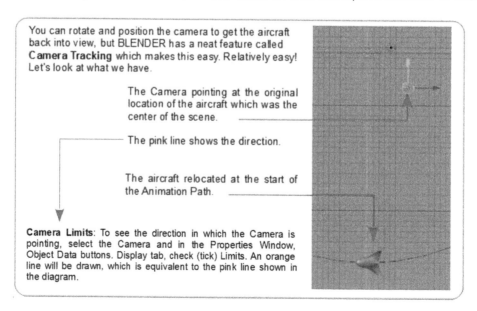

You can rotate and position the camera to get the aircraft back into view, but BLENDER has a neat feature called **Camera Tracking** which makes this easy. Relatively easy! Let's look at what we have.

The Camera pointing at the original location of the aircraft which was the center of the scene.

The pink line shows the direction.

The aircraft relocated at the start of the Animation Path.

Camera Limits: To see the direction in which the Camera is pointing, select the Camera and in the Properties Window, Object Data buttons. Display tab, check (tick) Limits. An orange line will be drawn, which is equivalent to the pink line shown in the diagram.

Track to Constraint

You follow the same procedure that was used to set the Follow Path Constraint except this time you select Track To in the Constraint options.

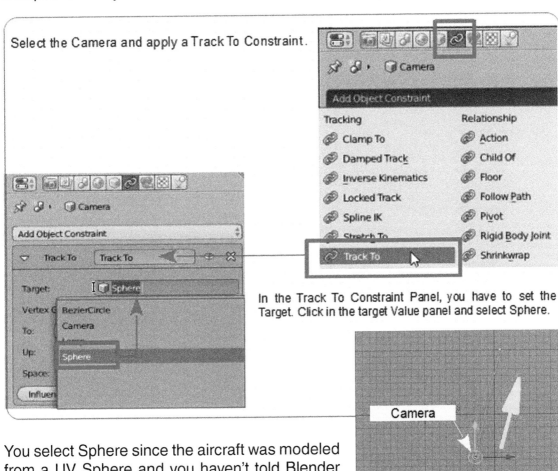

Select the Camera and apply a Track To Constraint.

In the Track To Constraint Panel, you have to set the Target. Click in the target Value panel and select Sphere.

Camera

You select Sphere since the aircraft was modeled from a UV Sphere and you haven't told Blender anything else.

In the 3D Window, you will see a dotted line connecting the Camera to the aircraft (Sphere). This shows that the Constraint is set.

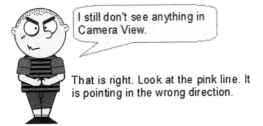

I still don't see anything in Camera View.

That is right. Look at the pink line. It is pointing in the wrong direction.

The Track To Constraint has been applied, but you have to reset the Camera's orientation.

In the Camera Constraint panel look at the To: and Up: values. Click on –Z (minus Z) for the To: value and change Z in the Up: value to Y (click on the Up: value panel and select Y in the menu).

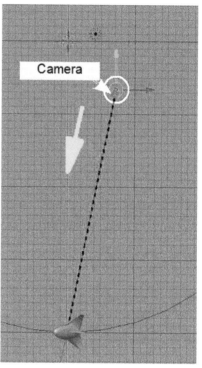

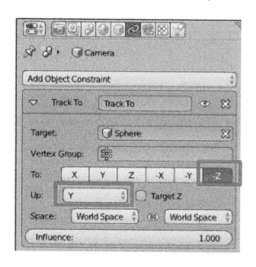

With the values set, the pink line is the same as the dotted line. You will see your aircraft in Camera View, but it is way way in the distance.

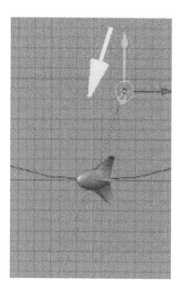

Grab the Camera and move it closer to the aircraft. It will remain pointed at the aircraft no matter where you position it. Playing the animation in Camera View will show the aircraft fly away and return. If the aircraft disappears from view at some point, it is because it moves out of range of the Camera.

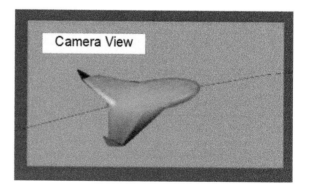

Chapter 13
Dynamic Paint

Dynamic Paint is one of several Physics applications in Blender. As the name indicates, this tool may be used for painting which in Blender is the application of Material (Color) to the surface of a Mesh Object. The tool does a little more than that however. It is also used for deforming the surface of a mesh.

To show you how the tool operates I will start with the paint.

Just like an artist painting a picture you will have a Brush to apply the paint and a Canvas on which to apply it. The Brush and Canvas can be any of the Blender Primitives, but to make the demonstration something like painting a picture on a Canvas, you will use a UV Sphere as the Brush and a Plane Object as the Canvas.

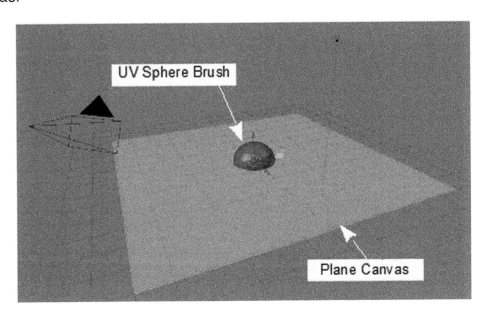

That's a weird sort of brush!

The Sphere is merely an Object representing a brush. It gives you something to grab and move over the surface of the Canvas.

To demonstrate Dynamic Paint, set up a Scene as shown in the diagram. There is a simple UV Sphere located at the center of the Scene in the center of the midplane. The sphere has a red Material applied. This is the Brush. The Plane is also located centrally and has been scaled up six times and in Edit Mode it has been subdivided six times. Subdividing adds vertices. Without sufficient vertices, you will not be able to paint. The Plane has also been given a pastel-colored Material.

Applying a Material (Color) to the Canvas or the Brush isn't necessary, it merely makes the demonstration more colorful.

To paint you have to set up Physics for the Brush and the Canvas. You will be using the UV Sphere Brush to paint on the Plane Object Canvas.

Physics is set up in the Properties Window, Physics buttons.

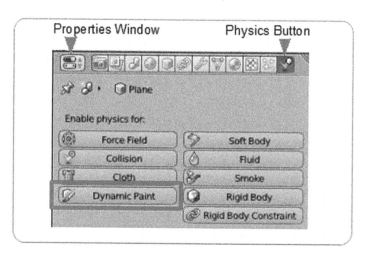

You will start with the Plane Canvas. Select the Plane in the 3D Window and in the Physics buttons click on Dynamic Paint.

The Dynamic Paint tab opens. Click on the Canvas button to apply Canvas properties to the Plane then click Add Canvas. The Dynamic Paint tab expands. Check (tick) Anti-aliasing and in the Frames: buttons change the Sub-Steps value to 1. Applying these values improves the output quality when painting.

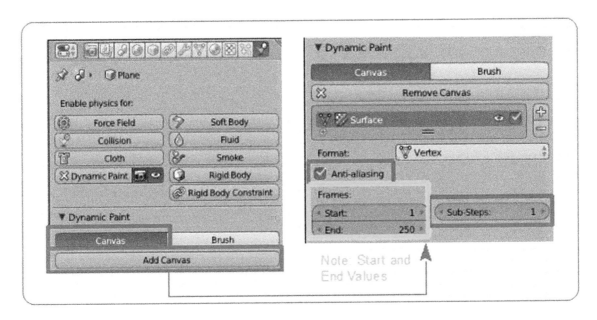

Now for the Brush. Select the UV Sphere in the 3D Window and again, in the Properties Window, Physics buttons click Dynamic Paint.

This time click on the Brush button then Add Brush. The Dynamic Paint Brush tab expands.

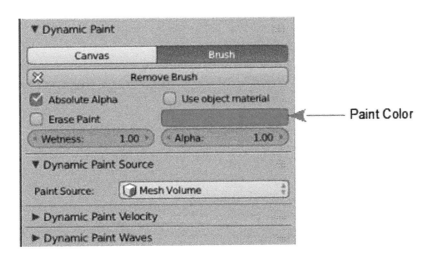

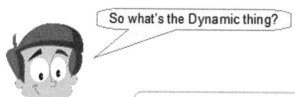

So what's the Dynamic thing?

Dynamic is defined as the way in which people or things behave and react to each other in a particular situation.

Here you go again, another definition which doesn't appear to have any relevance to what is happening. Well it doesn't until you understand the painting procedure. You are actually setting up to paint on the Canvas but if you were to grab hold of the Brush and thrash it about, nothing would happen.

There are two things you should know. The first is that the paint effect is created at the intersection between the Brush and the Canvas. In this particular case that will be at the center of the sphere since it is sitting with its center coinciding with the center of the plane in elevation. You select the Brush in the 3D Window, press the G Key (Grab), and move the mouse to paint.

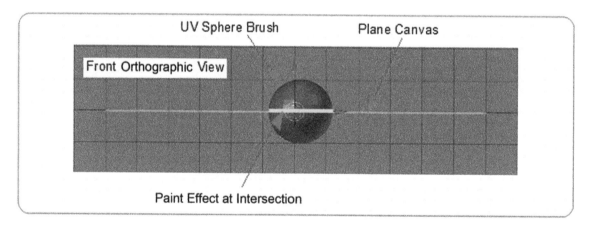

UV Sphere Brush   Plane Canvas

Front Orthographic View

Paint Effect at Intersection

The second point in regard to painting is since you have applied Physics, the paint action takes place while an Animation Sequence is running. This means that you have to activate or start the Animation in the Timeline Window before you can paint. You start the Animation by pressing the Play button in the Timeline Window or by pressing Alt + A Key on the keyboard.

If you have the 3D Window in User Perspective, User Orthographic, or Camera View, remember that moving the Mouse and dragging the Brush will translate it on the plane of the view. That is, it moves on the flat plane that is your computer screen. If the Canvas Plane is at a different angle then moving the Brush Sphere moves it away from the Canvas in elevation. To keep the Brush on the center of the Canvas in elevation, have the 3D Window in Top Orthographic View.

OK! Start the Animation sequence, grab the Brush, and move it (in Top Orthographic View). You will see the paint effect applied to the Canvas.

UV Sphere Brush Moved in a Circle

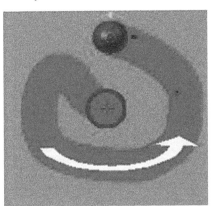

Animation Sequence Time

The default animation sequence in the Timeline Window is set to Start at Frame 1 and End at frame 250. The sequence runs for 250 Frames then repeats. The default Frame Rate is 24 frames per second (see the Properties Window, Render buttons, Dimensions tab—Frame rate). This means that, in order to paint, you have approximately 10 second to create your masterpiece.

You had better be a quick painter!

You can change the End Frame value in the Timeline Window in an attempt to increase the time but that doesn't do the trick. Go back and look at the Canvas Dynamic Paint tab in the Properties Window. Change the End Frame value here and in the Timeline Window.

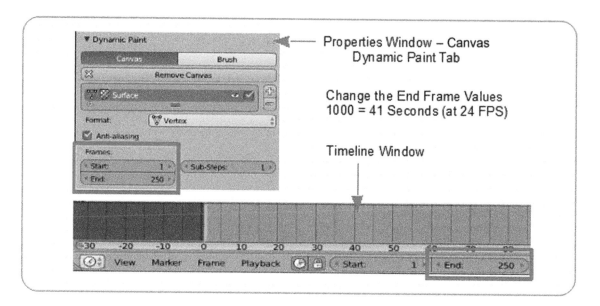

Brush Stroke Thickness

Obviously you may wish to vary the thickness of your paint line and obviously you can do this by increasing or decreasing the diameter of the sphere. Another way would be to use an inverted Cone Object as a Brush and vary its elevation in Front Orthographic View.

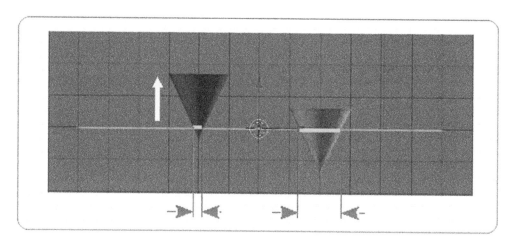

Paint Color

In the demonstration so far the paint color has been the default blue that you see in the color bar in the Brush, Dynamic Paint tab. Clicking on the color bar displays the color circle where you may select a different color.

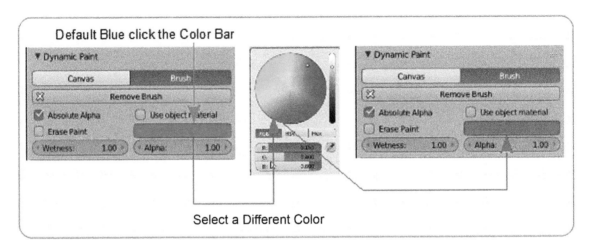

Default Blue click the Color Bar

Select a Different Color

Another option is to use the Material color of the Brush Object. Instead of clicking the color bar in the Dynamic Paint tab, check (tick) Use Object Material.

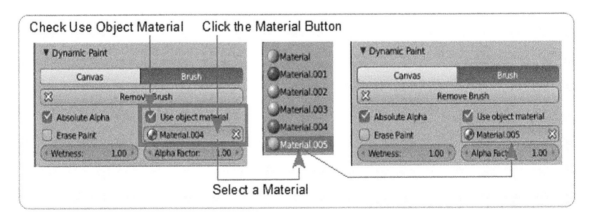

Check Use Object Material   Click the Material Button

Select a Material

The color bar will change to a Material Selection button showing the Material which is applied to the Brush Object. In the diagram above, the Material is Material.004.

Note: When you add or select Materials (Color) in Blender, the program stores the Material data in a Cashe. This provides a selection of predefined Material options from which to choose.

The color bar will change to a Material Selection button showing the Material which is applied to the Brush Object. In the diagram above, the Material is Material.004.

Can I paint my bike?

If you make a computer model of your bike, you can paint it whatever color you like. This would let you see if you like what you think you like before you go get the paint from the hardware store.

Drag the Brush around a side elevation of the Monkey Object to paint a stripe.

Experiment with other views and settings.

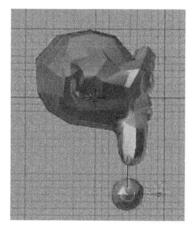

Dynamic Paint Is Not Just for Painting

There is more to Dynamic Paint than Paint. You can also use the tool to deform the surface of a mesh.

Set up a Scene as shown in the diagram. Yes it's the same as before with a UV Sphere in the center of a Plane which has been scaled up. **Don't forget to subdivide the Plane**.

I have applied a green blue Material to the Plane since we will be transforming the surface into water and making waves and ripples.

Set up the UV Sphere as the Brush. In this case, it is not necessary to apply a Material.

Set up the Plane as the Canvas, then in the Properties Window, Dynamic Paint Advanced tab click the Surface Type bar and select Waves from the menu.

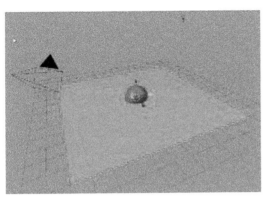

Click and Select Waves

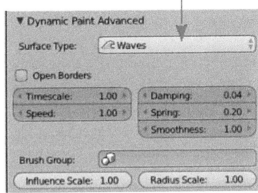

Click Play in the Timeline Window Header. Grab the UV Sphere Brush (G Key). Drag the mouse over the surface of the Canvas and see waves being made. It doesn't matter here that the Brush goes under or above the Canvas since this has the effect of producing splashes.

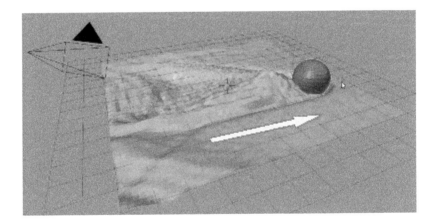

And there is still more. With the same set up as before, select Displace in the Dynamic paint advanced tab.

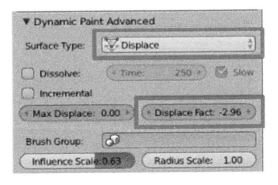

This time place the 3D Window in Top Orthographic View when painting. The surface of the Canvas (Plane) is deformed up or down depending on the Displace Factor value (– negative for depression + positive for elevation).

Note: If the negative–positive values work in the opposite direction, this is due to the Normals setting of the Canvas. Select the Canvas, Tab to Edit Mode and in the Tools panel Shading Uvs tab, under Normals, click on Flip Direction.

Rotate the 3D Window after stopping the Animation Sequence midway to see the effect.

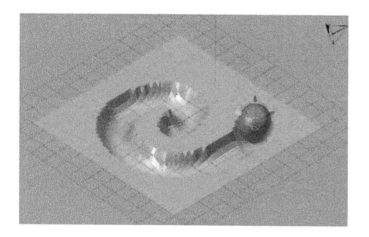

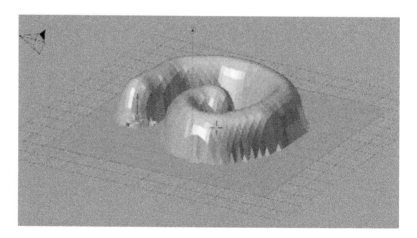

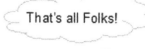

Chapter 14
Physics

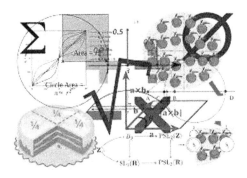

Physics is the study of matter and energy and the relationships between them, including the study of forces, heat, light, sound, electricity, and the structure of atoms.

In Blender, Objects are given Physics characteristics which make them behave how they would in the real world. This allows interaction with other objects when animated.

In a new Blender Scene arrange some Cubes, Planes, and a UV Sphere Object as shown in the diagram. The objective is to have the sphere roll down the inclined plane and knock down the stack of cubes. To do this, you assign Physics to each of the objects in the Scene.

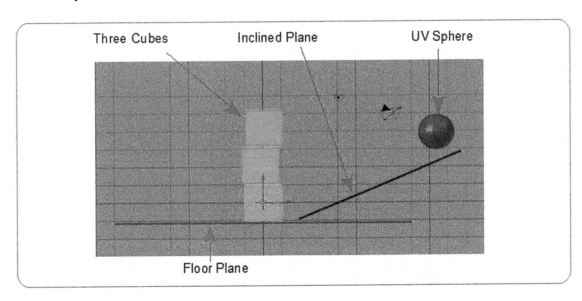

Three Cubes   Inclined Plane   UV Sphere

Floor Plane

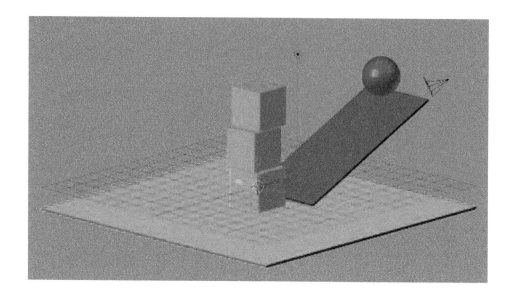

The arrangement doesn't have to be exact but pay particular attention to how the cubes are stacked. Position the bottom cube just above the floor Plane leaving a slight gap between the Cube and the Plane. Leave a slight gap between all the Cubes and have them slightly staggered.

Physics is applied to each Object in the Scene from the Properties Window, Physics buttons.

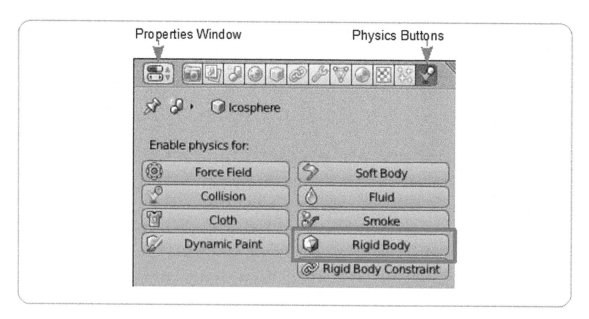

There are several options for enabling Physics but in this case use Rigid Body Physics.

To apply Physics to an Object, you must have the Object selected in the 3D Window. You do this for each Object.

Select the Floor Plane in the 3D Window.

In the Properties Window, Physics buttons click on Rigid Body. This applies Physics and opens the Rigid Body tabs. By default the Rigid Body Type is Active and Dynamic is checked (ticked).

You don't want the Plane to move in the Scene so change Active to Passive.

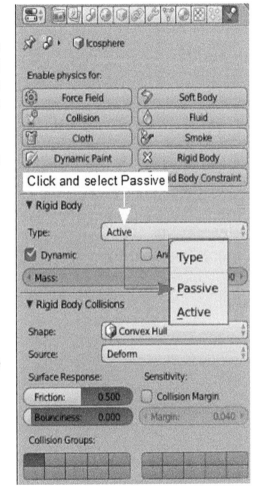

The Rigid Body tab Changes

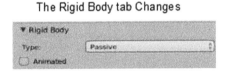

Repeat the same Physics set up for the Inclined Plane.

Set up Physics for the Cube Objects.

Select each Cube in turn and click on Rigid Body in the Physics buttons.

Now you want the Cubes to move in the Scene, therefore leave the Rigid Body Type: Active and ensure that Dynamic is checked.

Repeat the Active Dynamic Physics set up for the UV Sphere but in the Rigid Body Collision tab change Shape: from Convex Hull to Sphere.

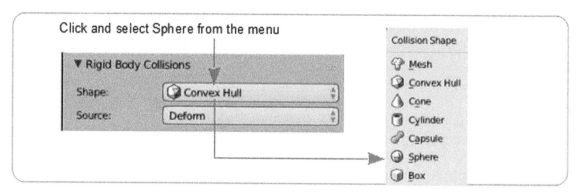

With Physics applied to all the Objects in the Scene, press the Play button in the Timeline Window. The Cubes will fall and sit on top of one another. The Sphere will roll down the inclined plane and give the cube stack a nudge. If you increase the Mass: Value in the Rigid Body tab to 10, the Sphere will demolish the stack and push two of the cubes off the side of the floor plane.

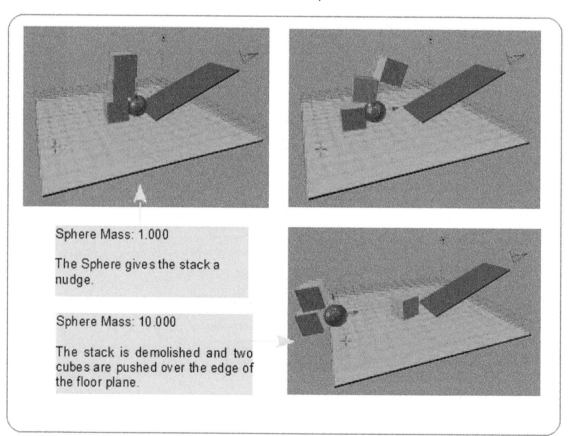

Sphere Mass: 1.000

The Sphere gives the stack a nudge.

Sphere Mass: 10.000

The stack is demolished and two cubes are pushed over the edge of the floor plane.

Other Physics Options

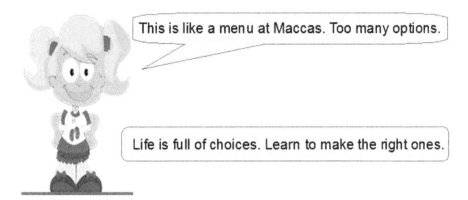

You have already used some of the other Physics options in your little Blender journey: Fluid, Smoke, and Dynamic Paint.

Take a look at the Cloth option. This one throws in a few variations in regard to the set up.

Start a new Blender Scene. Leave the default Cube Object where it is. Add a Plane Object. Scale the Plane up four times and subdivide it. **Don't forget to SUBDIVIDE!**

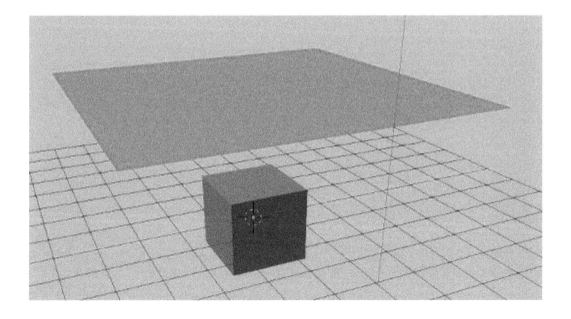

You may add a material (Color) to the Objects but it is not necessary.

The objective in this Physics exercise is to drape the Plane, which we will turn into a cloth, over the Cube.

Applying Physics in this instance is performed using Blender's Modifiers.

Select the Plane in the 3D Window then in the Properties Window, Modifier buttons click on Add Modifier and select Cloth from the menu.

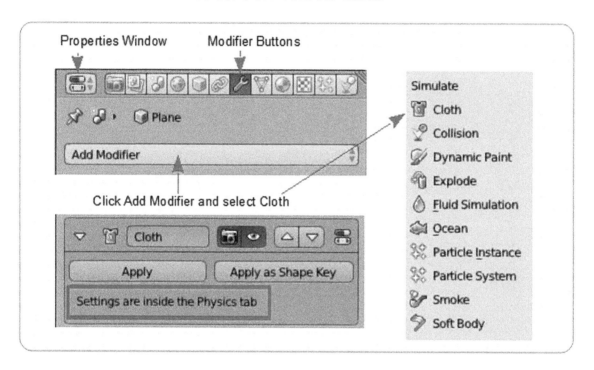

The Modifier is assigned to the Plane which turns it into a Cloth. You can see the Physics settings in the Properties Window, Physics buttons.

Select the Cube in the 3D Window then in the Properties Window, Modifier buttons click on Add Modifier and this time select Collision.

In the Timeline Window, press the Play button. The Cloth (Plane) falls and drapes over the Cube.

Pinning

Pinning means pinning the edges or corners of a cloth as if pegging to a clothes line.

Use the same Cloth arrangement with the Physics. In the Timeline Window, press the Go To Start button to position the Timeline Cursor at Frame 1.

Select the Cloth (Plane) in the 3D Window, tab to Edit Mode, press the A Key to deselect the vertices. Press Shift and RMB click two corner vertices.

Select two corner vertices

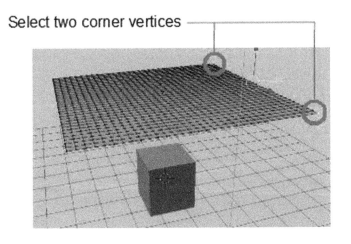

In the Properties Window, Data buttons, Vertex Group tab, click the Plus sign to create a Vertex Group Slot. With the two vertices selected in the 3D Window, click the Assign button to assign the two vertices to the Group.

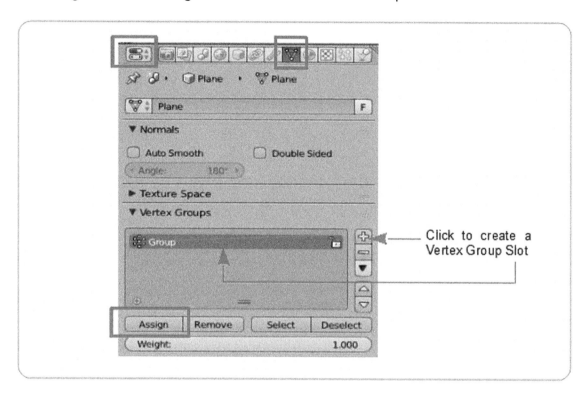

Click to create a Vertex Group Slot

Tab back to Object Mode.

With the Cloth (Plane) selected in the 3D Window, go to the Properties Window, Physics buttons, Cloth tab, and check (tick) Pinning. In the bar underneath, click and select, Group from the menu (Group is the only entry).

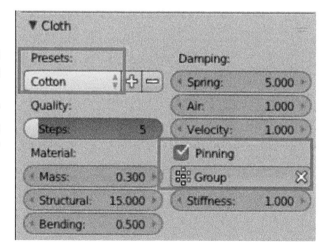

Click on the Presets: bar and select Cotton from the menu.

Press Play in the Timeline Window to see one side of the Cloth fall and drape over the Cube.

Note: The Cube tears through the Cloth. Go back and change the Presets to other options and see the different results.

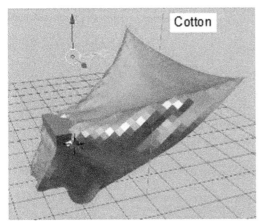

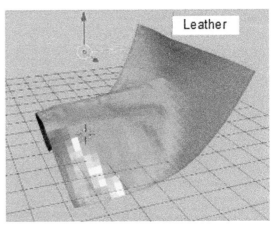

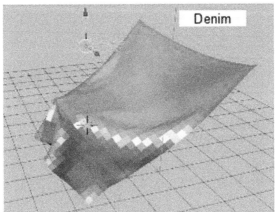

Chapter 15
Games

Can I make a video game in Blender?

The short answer is; Yes you can.

Game design is a whole book load of stuff in its own right so be prepared to head back to square one.

Blender has a special section built in for making games called the **Blender Game Engine**. In this section you place objects and characters in a Scene, which you can move, using the keyboard and mouse or a joystick. The moving objects are called **Actors**. The Actors interact with other Actors and Objects which you also place in the Scene. You can add special effects and animations to make the game really interesting.

The best way to learn how to make a game is to start from scratch (the beginning) so that you understand the basics. I can show you this, then you will be able to look at Blender Game files and figure out how they work.

Before you go into the Game Engine, you can make an Actor and a stage on which it performs, in the default Blender Scene.

I will keep this very simple, which means it won't be terribly exciting. This is the crawling stage which leads on to some really exciting stuff.

The Actor will be a simple Object which we will make move around in the Scene. You can use the default Cube Object. In the default Blender Scene, with the default Cube selected, scale on the Y axis as shown in the diagram. Tab into Edit Mode. In the Tool Panel (LHS of 3D Window) click on Subdivide once, to create more vertices. Select two center vertices and move them to form a pointy bit.

This is simply to allow you to see the direction of movement.

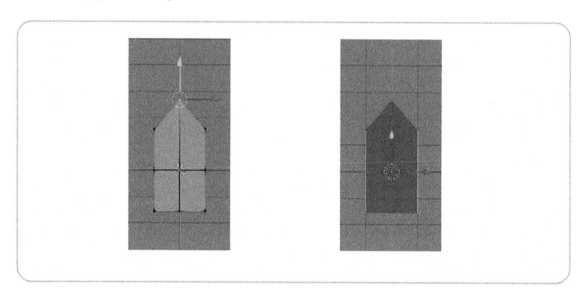

Tab back to Object mode and give the elongated Cube a Material color. Deselect the cube. Add a Plane Object, scale it up, and position it just below the Cube. Apply a Material to the Plane.

Remember that by default there is a Lamp and a Camera already positioned in the Scene.

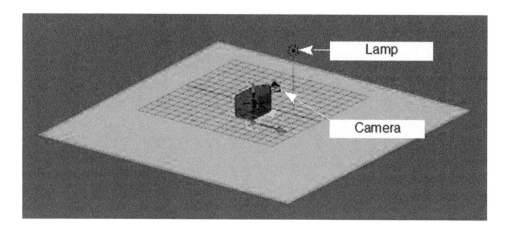

The Game Engine

To start the Game engine, there are two actions to perform. In the **Info Window** header at the top of the screen, click on the icon next to where you see **Default** and select **Game Logic** from the menu that displays. This changes the default Blender Screen arrangement, opening the windows for game development.

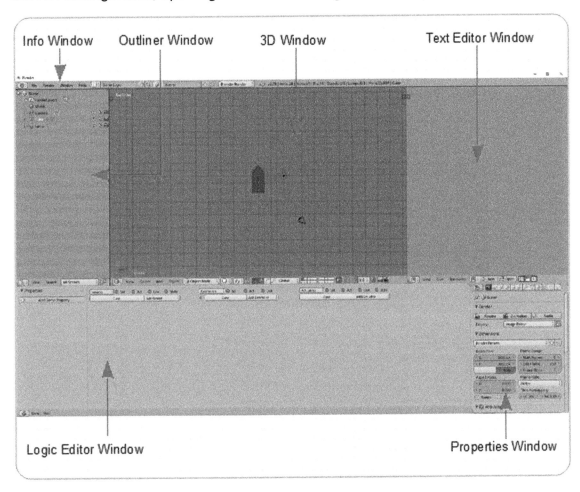

Info Window · Outliner Window · 3D Window · Text Editor Window

Logic Editor Window · Properties Window

In the **Info Window Header**, click where you see **Blender Render** and select **Blender Game** in the menu that displays.

The Logic Editor Window

The **Logic Editor Window** is where you assemble (program) the controls which make things happen in the game. The controls are programmed by assembling **Logic Blocks**. Logic Blocks are like icons which call up preassembled pieces of computer code. You don't have to write the code, you only have to understand what the pieces of code are for. At the top of the **Logic Editor Window,** you see the three selection panels for the Logic Blocks: **Sensor, Controller, and Actuator.**

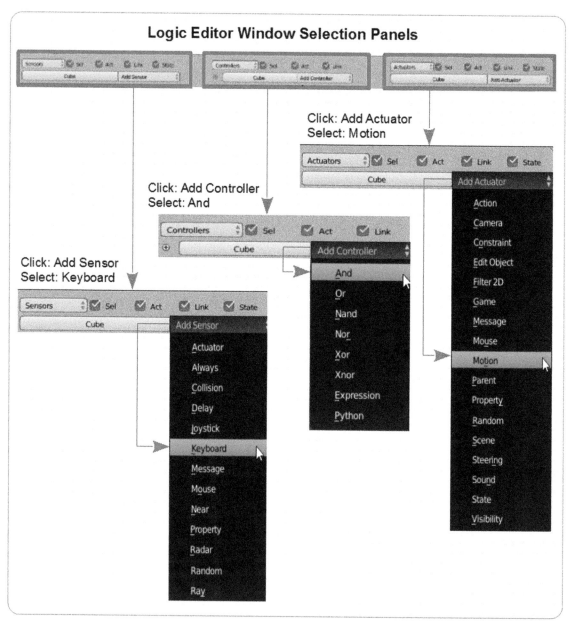

Sensors are the input signals which cause something to happen. These can be Mouse clicks or Keyboard buttons or actions from other objects.

Controllers, control how the Sensor signals are relayed to the Actuator.

Actuators have adjustable values which you set to make your Actor or Object behave in the game.

Clicking on the Add Sensor, Add Controller, and Add Actuator buttons displays menus for selecting different types of each category (see diagram opposite).

To understand how this works, create a Logic Block arrangement to drive your Actor (the elongated Cube with the pointy end) around in the Scene.

Make sure you have your Actor selected in the 3D Window.

Important: The Logic Block Assemblies you see in the window are for the Actor or Object that you have selected in the 3D Window. Different Actors or Objects have different assemblies.

Click on **Add Sensor** and select (click) **Keyboard** in the menu.

In the Keyboard Sensor that opens, click on the Key: panel. A message displays instructing you to Press a key. Press the W Key on your keyboard. This assigns the W Key as the input device for this sensor.

When you press the W Key, your Actor will move forward.

Well! It will eventually when you have finished setting up.

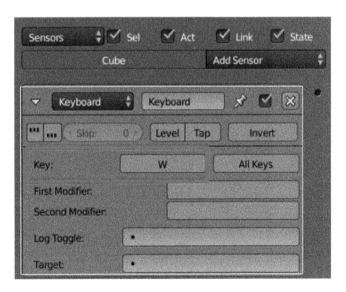

Logic Block Arrangement in the Logic Editor Window

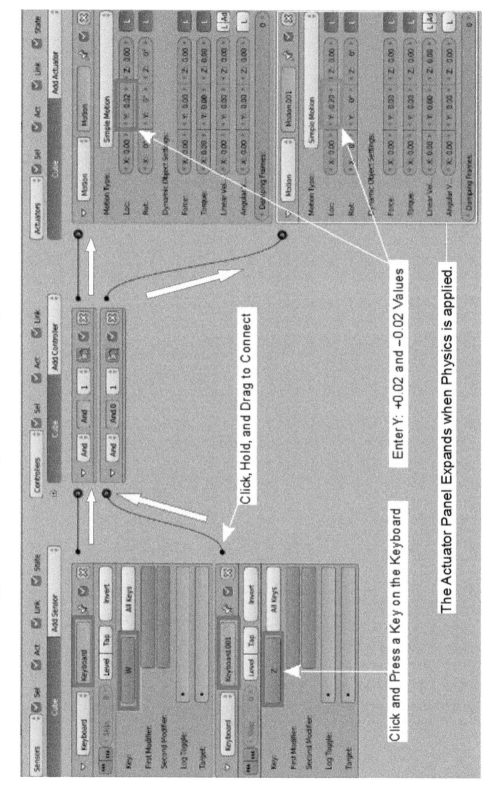

Click, Hold, and Drag to Connect

Enter Y: +0.02 and −0.02 Values

The Actuator Panel Expands when Physics is applied.

Click and Press a Key on the Keyboard

More Setting Up

Click on **Add Controller** and select **And** (Yes! **And**).

The And Controller is good to go as it is.

Click on **Add Actuator** and select **Motion**.

Note that in the Motion Actuator panel the Motion Type is **Simple Motion** and all the values for location (Loc:) and rotation (Rot:) are zero.

You will be hooking this Actuator up to the Sensor via the Controller. When you

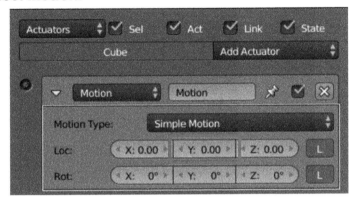

press the key you set as the input device for the Sensor (the W Key) you want your Actor to move in the forward direction. Forward is in the direction of the pointy bit. In the 3D Window in Top Orthographic View, you will see this as being positive along the Y axis. To get the Actor to move in a forward direction, set Loc: Y = 0.02 (0.02 is positive, −0.02 is negative which of course is the reverse).

With the Logic Blocks in place, click on the little black dot beside the Keyboard Sensor, hold, and drag over to the bigger black dot beside the And Controller. This is connecting them together and telling Blender to use the signal from one in the other. Do the same between the Controller and the Actuator.

Click on Add Sensor, Add Controller, and Add Actuator a second time, to add a second Logic Block for each category and repeat the connection process.

The diagram opposite shows the Logic Block arrangement for forward and reverse movement with the W Key as forward and the Z Key as reverse.

> Note: The Actuator panels look a little different to the one shown above. The panels have been expanded to include additional Dynamic Object Settings. These are added when Physics is applied to an Actor.
>
> Physics will be covered later.

Logic Block Arrangement for Forward–Reverse and Right-Left Rotation

Click on the Triangle to Collapse

See Previous Diagram

Keyboard Control Arrangement

You can assign any keyboard key you like as the input signal device, but it's a good idea to have a plan and make life as easy as possible for the game player.

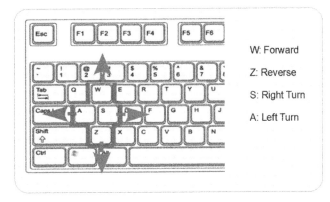

W: Forward

Z: Reverse

S: Right Turn

A: Left Turn

You want your Actor to move forward, reverse, and turn right and left. To make this happen, set up a pattern of keys on the keyboard which is easy to remember and easy to manipulate. Keep in mind that you may want to introduce other inputs such as a mouse click to cause something else to happen. One possible key pattern would be as shown above. This arrangement is shown on a Qwerty keyboard. Guess why?

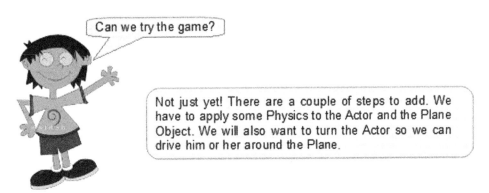

Can we try the game?

Not just yet! There are a couple of steps to add. We have to apply some Physics to the Actor and the Plane Object. We will also want to turn the Actor so we can drive him or her around the Plane.

As you can see in the diagrams, the **Logic Block Editor Window** rapidly begins to fill even though you have only worked on a simple forward and reverse motion. In the upper RH corner of each Sensor, Controller, and Actuator, you will see a small white triangle. You click on this to collapse and expand the panels.

Collapse the panels you have added so far, then add more Sensors, Controllers, and Actuators as shown in the diagram opposite. In the Keyboard sensor panels, assign the A Key and the S Key. When combined with the W Key and the Z Key, this provides a forward reverse and left and right configuration. *Note*: All Controllers are type **And.**

In the new Motion Actuators, enter **Ro**t (rotation) values of plus and minus 0.5 for the Z Rotation Axis.

When you finally get to try the game, you will find the forward and reverse motion is very slow. You can come back later and increase the values to whatever you wish, but we don't want you zooming off and crashing when you push the Play button.

Before you ask! No, you are not good to go just yet.

You have to assign **Physics**.

Physics gives the game components attributes which simulate how they behave in the real world.

Remember that by default, there is a gravitational effect applied in the Scene.

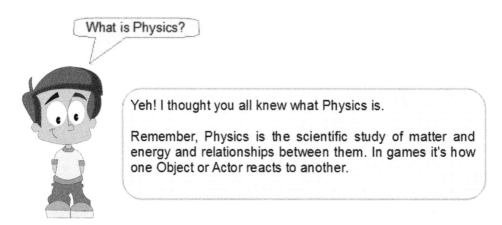

What is Physics?

Yeh! I thought you all knew what Physics is.

Remember, Physics is the scientific study of matter and energy and relationships between them. In games it's how one Object or Actor reacts to another.

Physics

As far as you are concerned, Physics is how an Actor or an Object reacts with other Actors or Objects in a Scene. Your Scene is an artificial world in which you are attempting to simulate the real world, therefore, there are physical forces built into the simulation. One of these forces is **Gravity**.

In Blender, Gravity is always in effect unless you turn it off. You can do this in the Properties Window, Scene buttons, but in case you forget, when an Object is entered in the Blender Game Engine it is designated as **Physics Type: Static**. This means it does not react to Gravity.

To apply Physics to an Actor or Object, have the object selected in the 3D Window, then in the Properties Window, click on the Physics button. The default Physics Type will be Static. The Actor or Object will not move when the game is played.

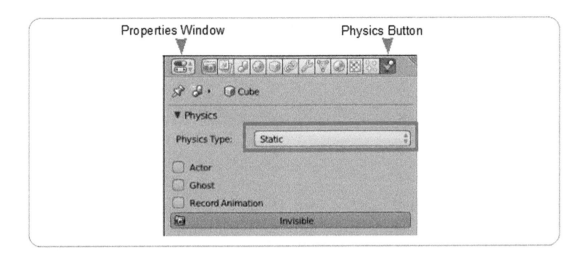

Properties Window   Physics Button

To change the Physics Type to Dynamic, click on the Physics type bar and select Dynamic from the menu. Set the Actor Physics Type to **Dynamic** and the Floor Plane to **Static.**

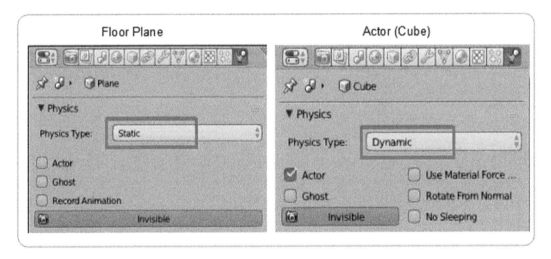

Floor Plane   Actor (Cube)

Can we play the game now?

Ok! Ok! You are good to go.

Press the P Key on the Keyboard.

When you start something it's a good idea to know how to stop it. To STOP the game, press the Esc Key.

To **STOP** the Game, press the Esc Key.

| 3D Window Mode | Game Mode |

In your very simple game, when you press the P Key, the game starts and you will see the Cube Actor fall and come to rest on the surface of the Plane.

To drive the Cube Actor around the Plane, press the W Key to go forward, the Z Key to reverse and A and S Keys for turning left and right. With the Y axis Loc (Location) values in the Motion Actuators set at 0.02, the forward and reverse movement will be very slow. When you have the feel for how the game is played, go back and increase the values.

A point to remember is the Axis values are the Local Axis values for the Object, not the Global Axis of the Scene. When you rotate the Cube Actor, the positive Y axis of the cube is in the direction of the pointy end.

This is the very basic assembly of a game in the Game Engine. From this point on, you can begin to build a game which will be much more interesting. As a starter, add more Cubes to the Scene positioned at random on the Plane. Give them Dynamic Physics then you can either drive around them or push them about on the plane.

If you drive the Actor off the Plane or push an Object over the edge of the plane, you will see them descend in space and disappear into oblivion. You may wish to include this feature in your game.

The Scene in Game Mode with Additional Objects.

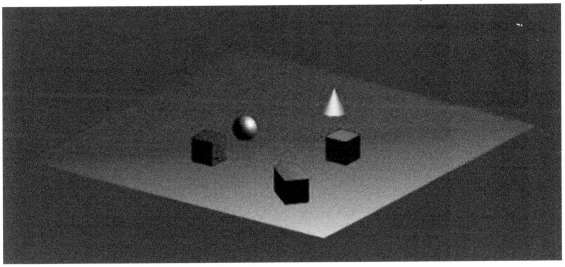

The Actor has been driven into the near corner of the plane.

Let's develop the game a little further.

Expand the 3D Window so that you have a good overall plan view of the Scene.

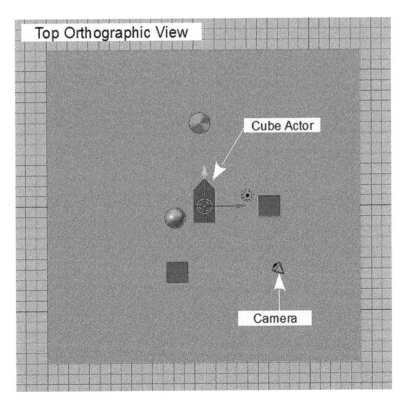

If you press the P Key (Play) with the Mouse Cursor in the window, the game will play in the view that is displayed in the 3D Window. In this case, in Plan View, press Esc to cancel Play.

Change to Camera View (Num Pad 0). Pressing P for Play in Camera View plays the game in Camera View. Remember, you must have the Mouse Cursor in the 3D Window before pressing the P Key.

It's all very well playing the game as if you are looking down from above but I know you will want to play from a first person perspective. That means you play as if you are sitting in the driving seat or looking from behind the gun in a shoot-em-up game. To do this, you position the Camera to look from behind your Actor and make the Camera move with the Actor.

In the Scene at the moment, the Camera View looks like the image on the left. You want to see it like the image on the right.

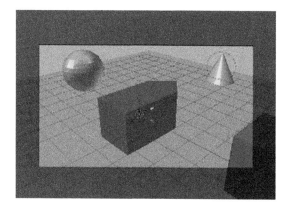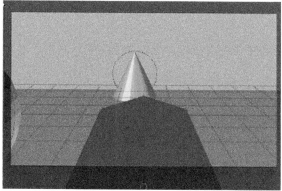

In the 3D Window, in Top Orthographic View, select the Camera and using the Widget move it in line with and slightly behind the Cube Actor.

Switch between Top view and Camera view and adjust the camera position until you have a view as shown in the right-hand image.

Pressing Play at this point and pressing the forward motion button (W Key) will see the Cube Actor move away from you heading toward the blue Cone.

The next trick is to make the Camera move with the Actor so that, from your point of view, you move with the Cube Actor.

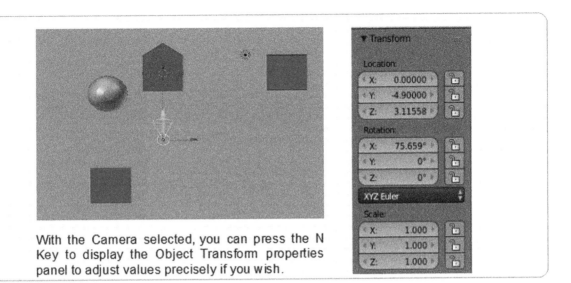

With the Camera selected, you can press the N Key to display the Object Transform properties panel to adjust values precisely if you wish.

Head down to the Properties Window which is in the Game Logic window arrangement, located in the lower RH corner of the screen.

Have the Cube Actor selected in the 3D Window. In the **Properties Window**, click on the Object data button, and in the Transform tab, check that all Rotation values are 0 and all Scale values are 1.000. When you model your Actor, you will inevitably start with one of the Blender Primitives and, depending on the complexity of the model, scaling and rotation will be performed. Residual values may remain after these operations. In your case you scaled the Cube Object on the Y axis. Do you see the scale value in the Transform tab? The rotation of the cube was unaltered.

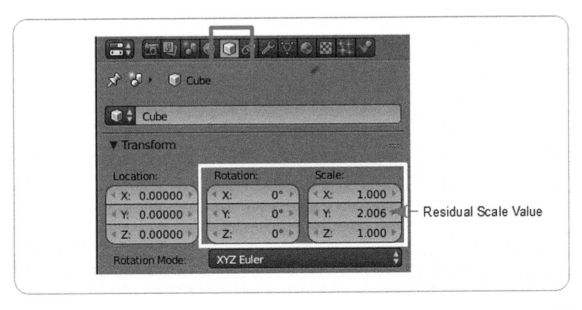

To have the Camera follow the Cube Actor, you have to Parent it to the Cube. This is like telling the Camera to take hold of the Cube's hand and not let go. Before you do this, you have to get rid of any residual scale and rotation values.

To remove the values, have the Cube Actor selected, then in the 3D Window header, click on Object, click on Apply, then select Rotation & Scale. This tells Blender to consider your Actor model as if it were a new Object which hadn't been messed with.

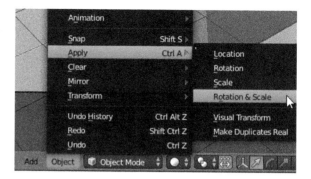

You now are set to Parent the Camera to the Actor.

Deselect the Cube Actor and select the Camera (press A Key to deselect and click RMB to select). In Camera View, you may click RMB on the edge of the camera aperture.

Note that the Properties Window changes to show the Object data settings for the Camera. In the Relations tab, click in the Parent bar with the little orange cube icon and select Cube from the menu that displays.

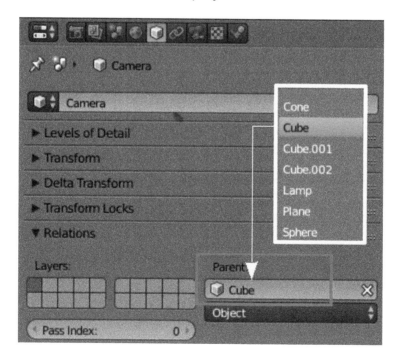

Remember: Cube is the name of your actor as far as Blender is concerned. The little orange cube in the Parent bar has nothing to do with this. It is merely an icon. If you had renamed your Actor something else and had modeled the Actor from one of the other Primitives, you would still see a cube icon.

With the Mouse Cursor in the 3D Window, Camera View, press the P Key (Play). The Objects in the game settle on the floor plane and when you press the W Key (forward motion) the Camera view follows the Cube Actor toward the Cone. Pressing the A, S, and Z Keys will direct the Cube Actor in the Scene.

Remember: If you drive the Cube Actor over the edge of the ground plane, it will disappear into oblivion.

How do we find out how to do more stuff?

At the beginning of the chapter I said the Game Engine was a book in itself. There are books devoted to the subject, but there are also hundreds of tutorials on the internet which give you instruction.

You will find excellent Game Tutorials at: Blender Free Movies.

www.blender.freemovies.co.uk/game engine/

Chapter 16
Project
Animation Sequence

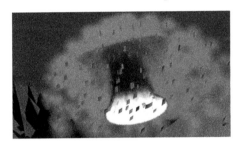

Having worked through the book, you will have picked up a fair amount of knowledge and discovered some of Blender's secrets. Blender is full of things to discover which are interesting as stand-alone features. When you are aware of these, you can begin to let your imagination run wild and create wondrous computer graphics. The following exercise will give you a feel for how to combine and use the features. You will learn more detail, building on what has already been covered, and more importantly see how to build a more complex animation.

Animation movies, especially full length feature movies, are made up of many video sequences combined into video clips which, in turn, are combined into the final feature movie. Each sequence may combine a number of Blender's features to produce effects.

Start at the beginning. A good place to start.

Hang on! Before you start have a plan.

The simple plan for this project is to see how a **model** is **animated** to collide with another model causing both to **explode** and catch on **fire**.

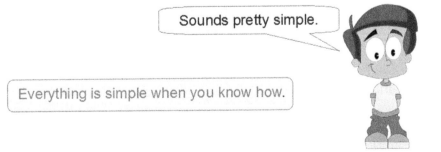

Sounds pretty simple.

Everything is simple when you know how.

It's obvious that the Blender features to be used are: Modeling, Animating, Explode (Quick Explode), and Fire (Quick Fire). These have been introduced in earlier chapters.

Guess what? You will be using the aircraft model from Chapter 5.

You did save the Blender **.blend** file, didn't you?

Start a new Blender Scene and delete the default cube.

The plan for the animation sequence is to have the aircraft appear from behind some hills, crash into a dome causing both the dome and the aircraft to explode. This is not intended to represent any event whether it be real or imaginary. It is merely a demonstration of creating something using animation effects.

In the demonstration I will be keeping to a fairly basic plan, therefore the end result will be a rather crude animation. In reality it would be a starting point for further refinement, but it will demonstrate how to combine the features.

The first step in the process is to create a background for the Scene.

Create a Landscape

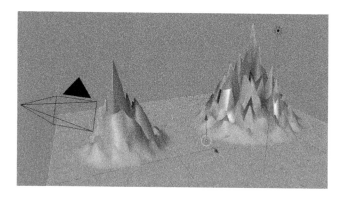

In the Scene, add a Plane object.

Scale the Plane up eight times (S Key + 8 + Enter). Tab into Edit mode, then in the Tool Panel at the LHS of the screen, click on **Subdivid**e, six times. This produces vertices for manipulation. Press the A Key to deselect the vertices.

Still in Edit mode, select a single vertex (click RMB) somewhere toward the rear of the Plane off to one side.

The Manipulation Widget will locate at the selected vertex. If it doesn't show, click on the Widget button in the 3D Window header. Also in the header, enable **Proportional Editing** and select the **Random Falloff** option.

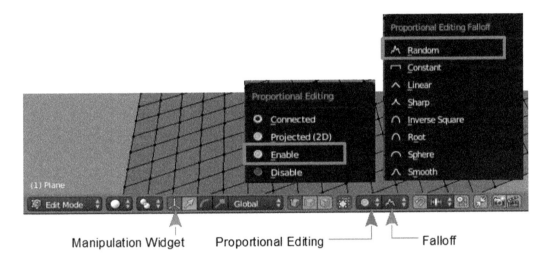

Manipulation Widget   Proportional Editing ———   ——— Falloff

With the single vertex selected, press the G Key (Grab). When you move your mouse, the vertex will move and a white circle displays. Scroll MMB to increase or decrease the circle size. This circle determines how many vertices will be affected by the **Proportional Editing**.

In adjusting the circle of influence, you will probably move some vertices about. For this exercise it is not important, but if you want to be precise, you can always press Ctrl + Z Key to undo previous steps in the editing.

Use the Widget to drag the vertex up (blue arrow). When you drag the selected vertex up, vertices within the circle of influence follow, and since you have Random Falloff selected they follow in a random order.

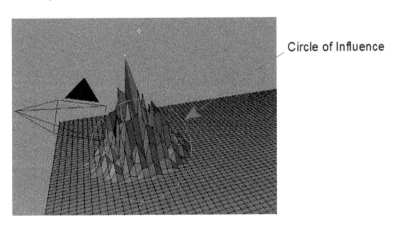

Circle of Influence

Press the A Key to deselect the vertex, then repeat the process on the opposite side of the Plane forming a second peak. None of this has to be precise since you want to create a random landscape. You may select several vertices at one time. Note that the vertices in the circle of influence are not selected as such. They just follow what is selected. You may also select vertices and move them down forming depressions in the landscape.

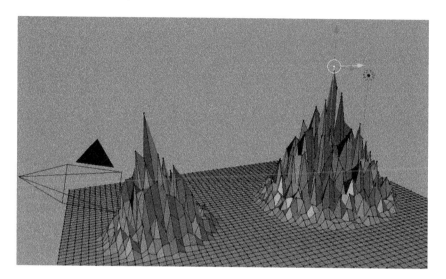

When you have your landscape shaped the way you want it, Tab back to Object mode. In the Tool panel, click on **Smooth**. In the Properties Window add a nice soft green Material color (see Chapter 7). I have used R: 0.600 G: 0.800 B: 0.432.

Deselect the Plane (Landscape). Press A Key.

Add a Dome to the Scene

Before you deselected the Plane, you would have seen the Manipulation Widget located at the center of the Plane. Since the Plane hasn't been moved, it remains at the center of the 3D World. The 3D Window cursor, however, could be anywhere in the window, wherever you happened to click the mouse button.

You are about to add a new Object to the Scene. When you add an Object, it will be placed at the location of the 3D Window cursor. To put the cursor exactly at the center of the Scene, press Shift + S Key and select **Cursor to Center** from the menu that displays.

Add a UV Sphere Object. Zoom in on the Scene and place the 3D Window in **Right Orthographic View** (Num Pad 1). The sphere is at the center of the Scene which is the center of the 3D World, therefore the lower half of the UV Sphere is below the Plane. To create a Dome, you simply remove the lower half.

With the UV Sphere selected, tab to Edit mode. In the 3D Window header, turn off **Limit Selection to Visible.**

Press the A Key to deselect the vertices, then the B Key (box select) and drag a rectangle around the lower half of the sphere. With the lower half selected, press the X Key and select **Delete—Vertices**.

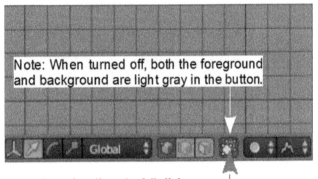

Note: When turned off, both the foreground and background are light gray in the button.

Limit selection to Visible

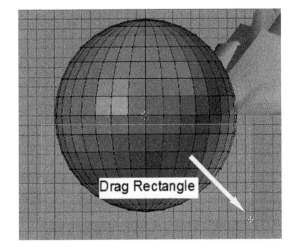

Drag Rectangle

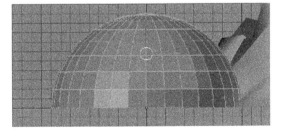

Lower Half Vertices Deleted

Change to Object mode and apply a Material (color) to the dome. I have used a Diffuse: R 0.800 G 0.080 B 0.002.

Add a Base to the Dome

Deselect the Dome (UV Sphere). In **Top Orthographic View** (Num Pad 7), add a Circle Object. Make sure the 3D Window cursor is at the center of the Scene which coincides with the center of the Dome. Press the S Key and scale the circle up slightly (S Key [scale]—Drag the mouse) so that you see it outside of the Dome. Tab to Edit mode. You will see the circle with vertices around its circumference.

Note: The center of the circle is empty (it has no surface). Press the F Key (Face) to fill in the center of the circle. Tab to Object mode and apply a Material (Black R 0.000 G 0.000 B 0.0000).

Note that the black circle coincides with the surface of the landscape in elevation. In either Front or Right Orthographic View, use the Widget and move the Circle up slightly.

You will have a red dome with a black base nestled into the side of the right hand mountain of the landscape.

It is time to add your aircraft model.

Add the Aircraft Model

Since your aircraft model is fairly simple, you can Append it from the Blender file that you previously saved. That is unless, like me, YES! me, you forgot to save it or you forgot where you saved it.

> No one is perfect. Everyone makes mistakes.
> An expert is someone who knows how to fix mistakes.

If you did forget, go back and start over. It's good practice.

OK! You have a model of an aircraft saved in a Blender file.

Append the model (see Chapter 9) into your new landscape.

Remember, the model will be entered at the location of the 3D Window cursor, so if the cursor is at the center of the Scene, which is the center of the Dome, your aircraft will Append inside the Dome. Depending on the scale, it may be completely hidden from view or it may stick out from the Dome.

Aircraft Model Appended into the Scene—Top Orthographic View

Scale the aircraft model down and park it off to one side in the Scene.

Make a note that your aircraft was modeled from a UV Sphere, so unless you renamed it, it remains named, Sphere, in your file. In this new Scene the Dome was modeled from a UV Sphere which was also named Sphere. You can't have two objects with the same name so Blender automatically will have renamed your aircraft model to Sphere.001.

At this point all the models for the animation sequence are in place in the Scene.

It's time for some animation.

Create a Glide Path

In Chapter 12 you animated your aircraft to fly around a circular path (a Bezier curve circle). This time use a Curve Path to create a glide path.

A Curve Path is a curve that can be shaped and extended to form a path that an Object can be made to follow in an animation.

Be in **Top Orthographic View** and locate the 3D Window cursor approximately as shown in the figure. When you enter a curve into a scene, it locates at the position of the cursor. Press Alt + A Key, select Curve then select Path.

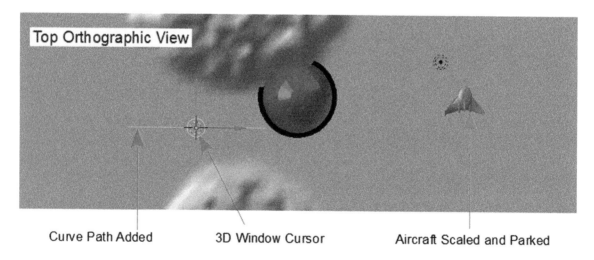

Top Orthographic View

Curve Path Added   3D Window Cursor   Aircraft Scaled and Parked

The Curve Path is entered in Object Mode and is positioned where you had the 3D Window cursor. In Top Orthographic View it will be as shown above, but in elevation it is at the center of the Plane forming the Landscape.

In Object Mode, in Front Orthographic View, move the Curve Path midway up the Dome.

Back in Top Orthographic View, Tab into Edit mode. You will see the path has chevrons along its length indicating the direction of travel an Object following the path will take. There is also a series of orange dots. These are **Control Points** for shaping the Curve Path.

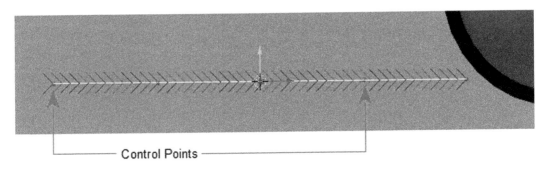

Control Points

With the Curve Path selected, tab to Edit Mode, then press the A Key to deselect the control points. The points will display as black dots. Click RMB on the LH dot then click and drag the green widget handle to curve the path. With the LH control handle still selected, press the E Key (extrude) and drag the mouse, extending the curve. Repeat the extensions (extrusions) forming a path around the mountain to a point approximately opposite the Camera.

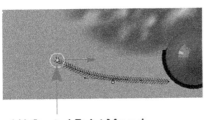

LH Control Point Moved

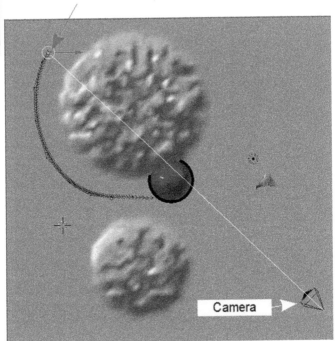

Last Control Point Opposite the Camera

Camera

Repeat the process with the other end of the Curve Path shaping and extending it through the Dome to a point somewhere off to the RHS.

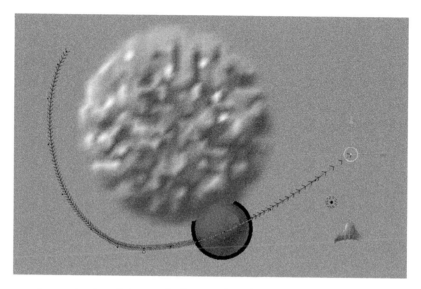

In elevation, grab control points and shape the Curve Path to approximate the glide path shown in the figure below. The Path passes through the Dome.

At this point, the Curve Path is passing between the mountain peaks.

At this point, the Curve Path passes through the Dome.

With the glide path complete, tab to Object mode and deselect the curve (A Key).

Animate the Aircraft

The aircraft model will be animated to follow the Curve Path.

Place the 3D Window in Top Orthographic View.

Select your aircraft model and move it over to the start of the Curve Path.

In the **Properties Window, Constraint button**, add a **Follow Path Constraint** (Chapter 12) with the **Target** set as **Nurbs Path** and with **Follow Curve checked** (ticked). If necessary, drag the aircraft to the start of the path and align by setting Forward: Y and Up: Z in the Constraint Panel.

Aircraft at the Start of the Curve Path

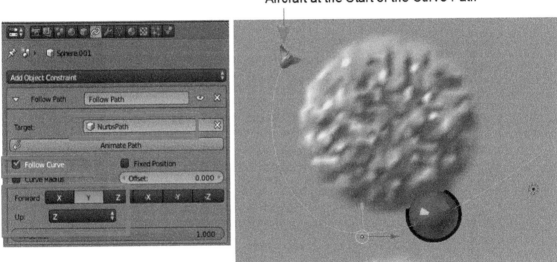

Deselect the Aircraft Model and select the Curve Path.

In the Timeline Window, the Timeline Cursor (green line) should be at Frame 1.

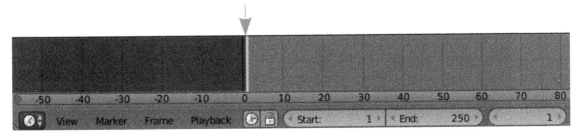

The Aircraft model is positioned at the start of the Curve Path and the Timeline Cursor is at Frame 1.

With the Curve Path selected, in the **Properties Window, Object Data button, Path Animation tab** ensure that **Path Animation** is checked (ticked). Click RMB on the **Evaluation Time bar** and select **Insert Keyframe** from the menu. The bar turns yellow and a yellow line is drawn at Frame 1 in the Timeline Window.

Click on the Timeline Cursor and drag it to Frame 250. In the **Evaluation Time bar** (it is displayed green), change the value to 100.000 (100%). Click RMB in the **Evaluation Time bar** and select **Insert Keyframe** from the menu.

When you changed the Evaluation Time to 100%, your Aircraft Model relocated to the end of the Curve Path.

Click on the **Go to Start** button in the Timeline Window header to position the cursor at Frame 1. Your aircraft relocates to the start of the Curve Path.

Press the **Play** button in the Timeline Widow to see your aircraft move along the path in the 250 frame animation.

The aircraft moves fairly slowly. To put the movement into perspective, imagine the aircraft is a huge jumbo jet flying around a mountain. The 250 frame animation is playing at the default 24 frames per second, therefore the aircraft takes approximately 10 seconds to traverse the path. In Camera view the Aircraft, as it appears from behind the mountain, swings around, and passes through the Dome.

You can click and drag the green Timeline Window cursor backward and forward to see how it looks at different frames. Do this and make a note of the frame number where the Aircraft sticks about half way into the Dome, and the frame number where it is sticking half way out when it exits. You will use this information a little later on.

Everything is fine so far so it's time to introduce explosions into the animation. The objective will be to have the Dome explode and catch on fire when the aircraft hits it, then the aircraft will also explode.

To introduce fire and explosion, use the Quick Smoke method (Chapter 2) in conjunction with an Explode Modifier (Chapters 3 and 4).

Exploding the Dome

Select the Dome in the 3D Window. In the Properties Window, Particles buttons, click New to add a Particle System.

Set the values as shown in the figure below.

Although the animation in the Timeline plays for 250 frames, Particles will only be emitted between Frame 146 (when the Aircraft just enters the Dome) and Frame 166.

The Explode Modifier works in conjunction with the Particle System; therefore, the explosion takes place in 20 Frames (0.83 seconds).

In the explosion the Faces of the Dome (UV Sphere) follow, the Particles. Particles will emit from the Volume in a random order.

The Normal value gives the Particles an initial velocity (speed) and the Z: 2.5 value directs the Particles in an upward direction which works against the force of gravity.

With the Dome selected add an Explode Modifier in the Properties Window, Modifier buttons.

Play the animation in the Timeline to see the Dome explode when the Aircraft crashes into it. You will see the Faces of the Dome fly away. Drag the Timeline cursor to a point just past the beginning of the explosion. Render an image (F12).

3D Window Camera View

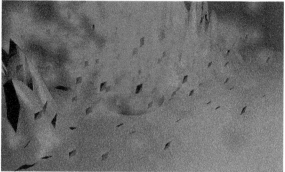
Rendered Image Press F12

You see that the rendered image is very different from the view in the 3D Window. The faces of the Dome fly apart following the particles. The particles render as points of light taking on the Material (color) of the Dome.

Look closely at the 3D Window view and you will see your aircraft inside the explosion, intact. In the animation, it flies through the Dome unscathed. This will be addressed later.

When something explodes, it can start a fire so you should add fire into the equation.

Adding Fire

After the Dome explodes, there isn't much left except for the base (the black circle). Add the Quick Smoke Modifier to the Circle.

Select the Circle object. Press the Space Bar and in the search window that displays type, **Quick Smoke**. In the Tool panel at the LHS of the window, set the modifier to **Type: Smoke + Fire**.

In the 3D Window, you will see an orange rectangle appear surrounding the Dome. This is the **Domain** for the **Smoke + Fire simulation**. It represents the cubic volume of space in which the simulation takes place. It only surrounds the Dome since the Circle object was placed at the base of the Dome. The size of the Domain could be adjusted to suit, but it should be fine the way it is.

Play the animation in the Timeline. Smoke and fire emit from the Circle immediately. To delay the emission until the explosion takes place, you must first let the animation play through to the end.

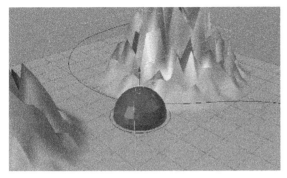

The Domain for Smoke + Fire

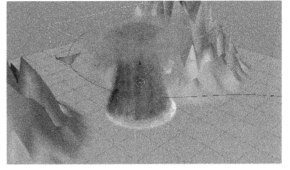

Smoke + Fire Simulation

Playing the animation creates the data for the Smoke + Fire simulation and stores it in a **Cache**. The controls for the Cache are in the Properties Window, Physics buttons, Smoke Cache tab. In the tab, set Start: 150 (the frame just after the explosion commences). Leave the End frame as 250. The fire will continue to the end of the animation.

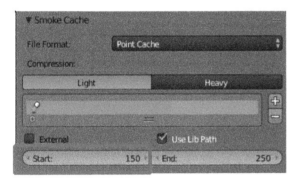

Smoke Cache

Rendered Image with Smoke + Fire

When you play the entire animation at this point, the Dome explodes and catches on fire when the Aircraft crashes into the Dome. Miraculously the Aircraft flies on by without a scratch. Of course, the Aircraft would also explode in the disaster.

Explode the Aircraft

To cause the Aircraft to explode, you perform a similar operation to exploding the Dome. Select the Aircraft, add a Particle System and an Explode Modifier.

In the Properties Window, Particle buttons, Emissions tab set Start: 170 (midway into the explosion), End: 190 (190 − 170 = 20 divided by 24 frames per second = 0.833 seconds). Set Emit From: Volume, uncheck Even Distribution and change Jittered to Random.

191

Play the animation to see the Dome explode, catch on fire and the Aircraft disintegrate leaving the fireball. Change the Material of the Aircraft to something dark (dark blue) for a better view.

Exploding Aircraft

What's This?

The rectangular shape in the render is a shadow from the Domain. To stop this occurring go to the Properties Window, Render buttons, and uncheck Shadows in the Shading tab.

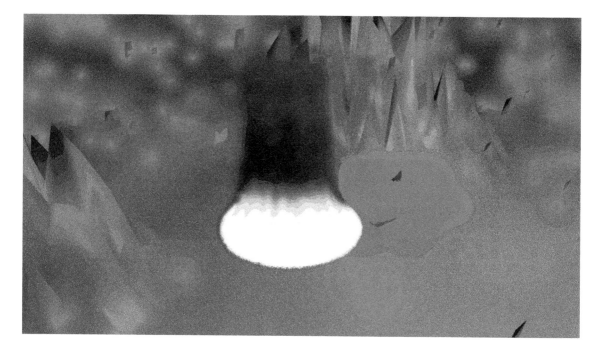

The End.

This exercise demonstrates how features in Blender are combined to produce an effect. The animation produced is rough around the edges and could do with refinement but it will do for now.

As you will have seen, there are numerous settings, which can be combined and adjusted to suit an application. This is the world of computer graphics. It is a fantastic study and I hope this introduction encourages you to explore and discover other fantastic features.

Chapter 17
Installation

Installation is as easy as ABC.

Remember learning ABC? Probably not, but when you start out the simplest things aren't that easy. Sometimes everyone assumes that you know how to do stuff and it's not always easy to remember.

I will run through this installation business from go to whoa.

Hook on to the Internet and use your web browser to go to the Blender website:
www.blender.org

If you type: www.blender.org/downloads/ into the web address bar, you will arrive directly at the download page.

Either way you will arrive at the download page and be presented with choices for downloading, for Windows, Mac OX, or GNU/Linux. These are operating systems so you download the Blender version which is suitable for the system you have on your computer.

I will run through the download and installation for a Windows operating system.

Even for Windows you are presented with more choices such as a download for a 64-bit system or a 32-bit system (see the note at the end of the chapter). Again you download the version for the system you have on your computer. Then you have options for downloading from various locations. DE is from Germany and NL1 or NL2 are from the Netherlands. You can choose whichever is best for you depending on where you live.

Download Blender 2.77

Blender 2.77 is the latest stable release from the Blender Foundation.
To download it, please select your platform and location. Blender is Free & Open Source Software.

Blender 2.77 was released on March 19, 2016.

Read about the new features and fixes in the Blender 2.77 Features page.

Blender 2.77 for Windows Compatible with Windows 10 | 8 | 7 | Vista	64 bit	32 bit
Installer (.msi)	DE NL 1 NL 2	DE NL 1 NL 2
.ZIP	DE NL 1 NL 2	DE NL 1 NL 2

ⓘ Windows XP is not in (active) support anymore.
If Blender reports an error on startup, please install the Visual C++ 2013 Redistributable Package. Click here.

Still more choices. Do you want an **Installer (.msi)** file or a **.ZIP** file?

You choose the options by clicking in the download window.

Installing with the Installer (.msi) Option

If you choose the Installer (.msi) option, you will be presented with this download window:

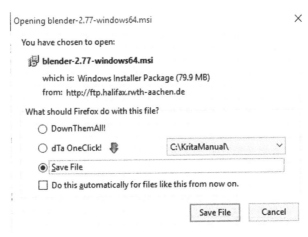

Note the diagram shows the Windows installer for a 64-bit system. Click on Save File to download to your computer. You will probably find the download in your Downloads folder:

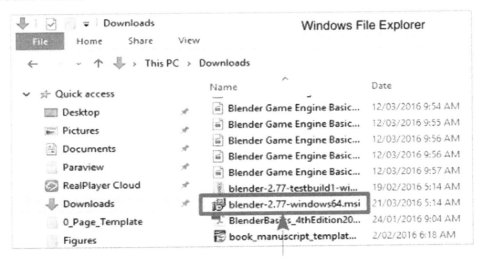

Double click on the file name in the Downloads folder and Blender will be automatically installed to the Program Files folder on your computer and an icon will be placed on your Desktop.

Installing with the .ZIP Option

If you chose the .ZIP option, you will be presented with this download window:

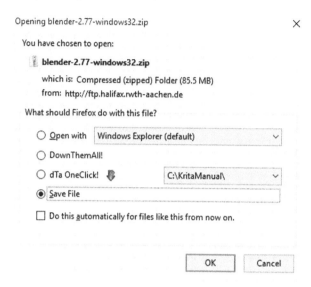

Note: In this case the diagram shows the download for a 32-bit system. Click on OK to save the file to download it to your computer.

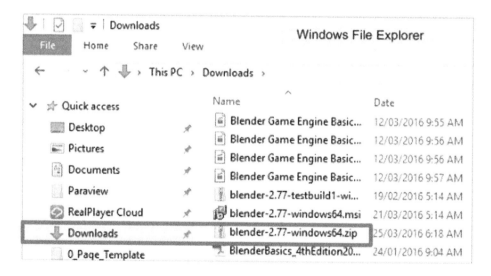

With a .ZIP file, you will have to unzip the file. You first create a new folder on your computer, then use a program like 7-Zip or Win-Zip to unzip (decompress) the zip file into the new folder (see the note at the end of the chapter).

When the file is unzipped into the new folder, you will see **blender.exe** as one of the entries. You double click on this to run Blender or you can create a shortcut which places an icon on your desktop.

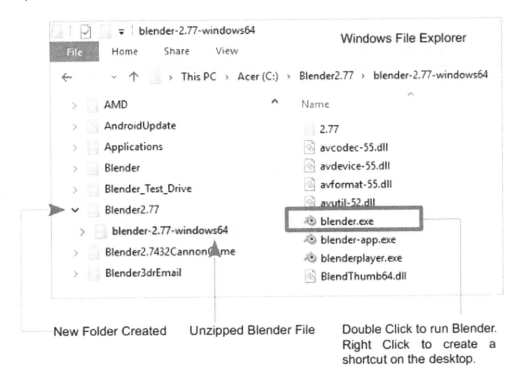

New Folder Created   Unzipped Blender File   Double Click to run Blender. Right Click to create a shortcut on the desktop.

Note: 32–64 Bit

The terms **32 bit** and **64 bit** refer to the way a computer's processor (also called a CPU) handles information. The **64-bit** version of Windows handles large amounts of random access memory (RAM) more effectively than a **32-bit** system.

Note: Unzipping

7-Zip is an open source (free) application for decompressing (unzipping) .zip files. You download the program from: http://www.7-zip.org where there is a link to 7-Zip's Source Forge web page which provides instructions.

Chapter 18
Blender Overhaul

Now that you have taken the test drive and found out some of what Blender can do, you might like to take a closer look under the hood and discover more about the program.

You have probably crashed through a few gears and encountered problems during your drive so you will need the manual before you start tinkering.

Every good mechanic has a check list to follow when they do an overhaul or a service on a vehicle. With Blender, the check list for the major parts is the list of windows that are available.

The Windows are listed as **Editor Types,** and the list is accessed by clicking on any of the window icons.

For example, click on the 3D Window icon or on the Info Window icon.

3D View: This is the **3D Window** where you create models and scenes. The 3D Window has several different Viewport Shading modes which control how the Scene in the windows displays.

The Shading Mode you select depends on what you are doing at the time.

The 3D Window also has different operational modes, which, again, are selected depending on the operation being performed. You have seen how to switch between Object Mode and Edit Mode.

Pressing the Tab Key toggles (switches) between Object and Edit Mode.

The other options are selected for specific operations.

Timeline: The **Timeline Window** where you construct and play animations.

Graph Editor: The Graph Editor Window has two different modes.

F-Curve: When an Object is animated to move in a scene, graphs are displayed in this window mode. The Graphs are editable; therefore, the animation (movement of the Object) can be controlled by changing the graph.

Driver: Drivers are another way to control animations.

Dope Sheet: The **Dope Sheet Window** also has several different modes for a variety of operations.

NLA Editor: The **NLA Editor Window** is primarily used for animation control.

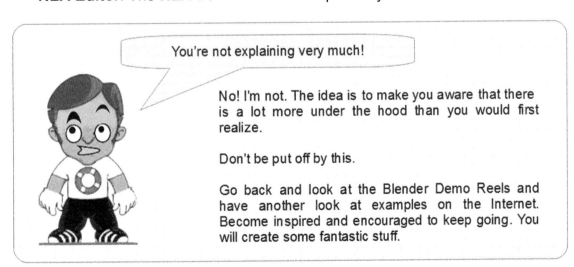

UV Image Editor: The **UV Image Editor Window** is, as it says in the name, where you edit images. There are modes for painting and creating image masks.

Video Sequence Editor: Video editing tools.

Movie Clip Editor: Motion tracking tools.

Text Editor: Where you can write notes or edit code.

Node Editor: There is a fantastic way of adding and controlling Materials (colors) and Textures. Preassembled code is displayed in graphic blocks called Nodes. These blocks can be arranged and connected together in a multitude of ways to produce an infinite array of effects.

Logic Editor: This window was demonstrated when we discussed Game Creation. It's where you set up the controls for your video games.

Properties: The Properties Window. The power house with all the buttons and sliders for controlling most everything in the 3D Window.

Outliner: The **Outliner Window** shows you a display of everything in the 3D Window. Sometimes, when an Object is obscured by other things in the window which prevent you selecting what you want, you can select it here.

User Preferences: The User Preferences Window. This is where you change Blender and make it look the way you want. We saw how to change the background color of the 3D Window.

Info: The Info (Information) Window. If you drag the edge of the window down the screen you will see a line-by-line record of the actions you are doing in the 3D Window.

File Browser: The File Browser Window. As you have seen, this window opens when you want to find a picture you have saved to your computer.

Python Console: You see the Python Console flash on the screen when you start Blender. Python is the computer programming language used by Blender. The Python Console is the command line window for using Python.

As you can see, there are lots of windows with lots of options which means there is lots to learn and lots and lots of stuff you can do.

Conclusion

Blender is a fantastic program and computer graphics is an intriguing subject, which you can pursue as a hobby or a profession. This book has merely given a brief test drive in the Blender world. There is much more. It is impossible to write a book which covers all that there is to learn. If you wish to continue studies in Blender, there are numerous publications which cover specific parts of the subject, and there are literally hundreds of websites which provide video tutorials on all sorts of topics.

I recommend my book *The Complete Guide to Blender Graphics*.

Supplemental material may be found on the companion website, www.silverjb.limewebs.com

The Complete Guide to Blender Graphics is a manual designed for those who wish to undertake a learning experience and discover a wonderful creative new world. **The book will help you with the basics of computer animation using Blender**. My approach has been to introduce the Blender features with examples and diagrams referenced to the graphical user interface (GUI).

In *The Complete Guide to Blender Graphics*, I reference video tutorials presented by Neai Hirsig of Tufts University, Boston.

Blender 3D Design Course

http://www.gryllus.net

Other excellent websites are:

Sardi's Blender Tutorials

https://www.youtube.com/user/srf123

Blender Guru

http://www.blenderguru.com/tutorials/

and of course

The Blender Website

https://www.blender.org/support/tutorials/

Blender Free Tutorials

http://www.blender.freemovies.co.uk

B3D101 Tutorials for Learning 3D

b3d101.org/en/learn/

Index